# THE BIG BOOK

## OF

## HOW TO DRAW FOR MINECRAFTERS

## A Step by Step Easy Guide

### (COLORIZED VERSION)

# Mark Mulle

Do you want to learn how to draw Minecraft stuff?

This guide will show you how to draw 50 different mobs, tools and other stuff from Minecraft starting from scratch to its final details. Some of the characters and items are easy to draw and some are a little challenging, but as you will discover in the book everything starts from squares and lines. So as long as you can draw squares, circles and lines you'll be able to draw these awesome stuff.

So what are you waiting for?
1. Sharpen your pencil
2. Get your paper
3. Have an eraser too to erase errors and to remove line guides
4. Grab your crayons so you can also color your masterpiece
5. and last of all Have fun!!!

# STEVE

## DIFFICULTY LEVEL

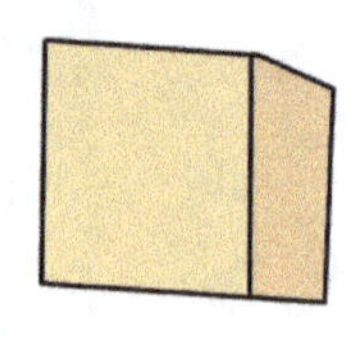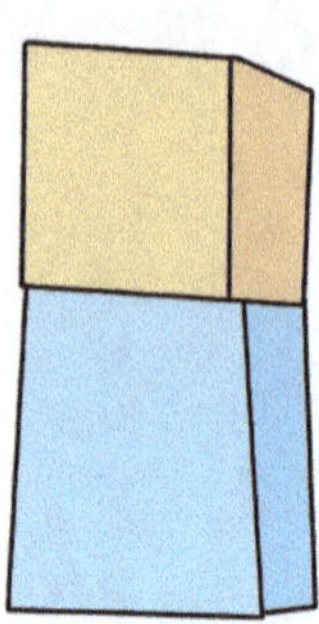

**1** FIRST DRAW THE SHAPE OF STEVE'S HEAD AND TORSO.

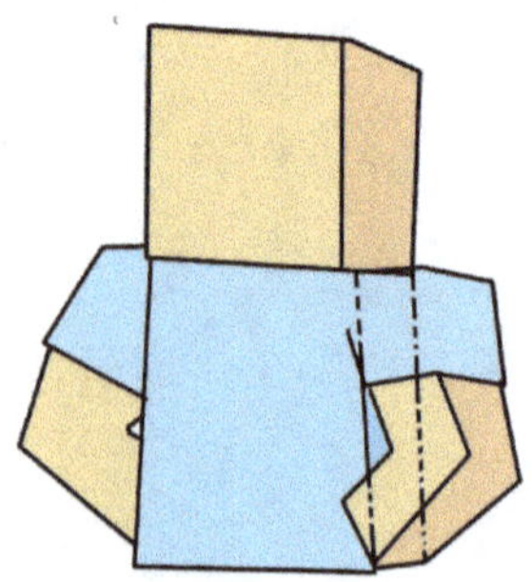

**2** DRAW HIS HANDS. ERASE DOTTED LINES.

**3** NEXT STEP IS EASY JUST FOLLOW OUR LEAD. DRAW HIS LEGS.

**4** ALMOST DONE! NOW WHEN YOU HAVE THE SHAPE OF STEVE'S BODY USE THICKER LINES TO DRAW HIS FINAL SHAPE..

**5** FEW MORE DETAILS AND OUR STEVE IS DONE! ADD HIM A FACE, SOME SHADING AND HE IS READY.

# MOOSHROOM

## DIFFICULTY LEVEL

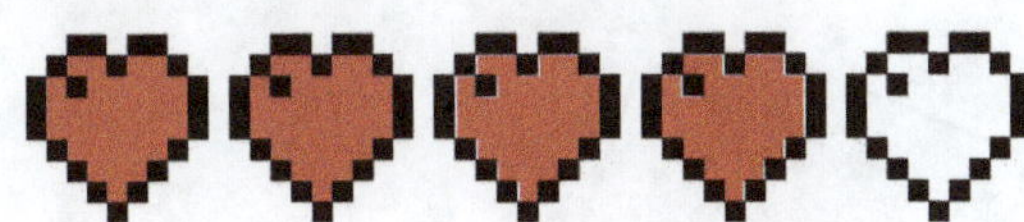

**1** FIRST DRAW CUBE FOR MOOSHROOM'S HEAD AND ADD ITS EARS AND SNOUT.

**2** NEXT DRAW TORSO

**3** NOW DRAW ITS LEGGS

**4** ALMOST DONE, NOW YOU HAVE THE SHAPE OF THEMOOSHROOM, JUST ADD ITS TAIL.

**5** ADD FACE FEATURES, SPOTS, MUSHROOMS, AND SOME SHADING AND YOU ARE DONE.

# SQUID

## DIFFICULTY LEVEL

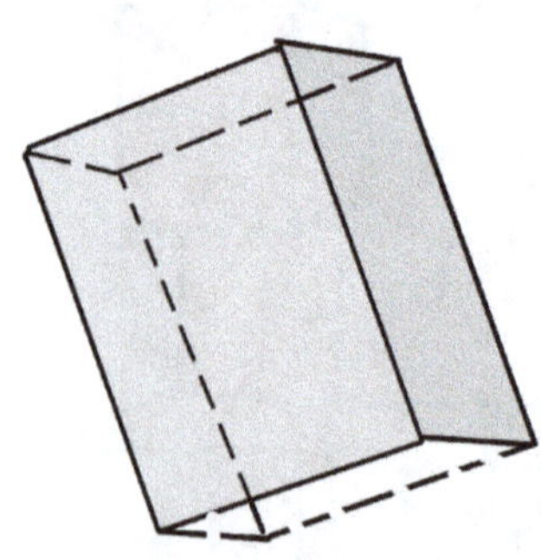

**1** FIRST DRAW THIS SHAPE FOR SQUID'S HEAD.

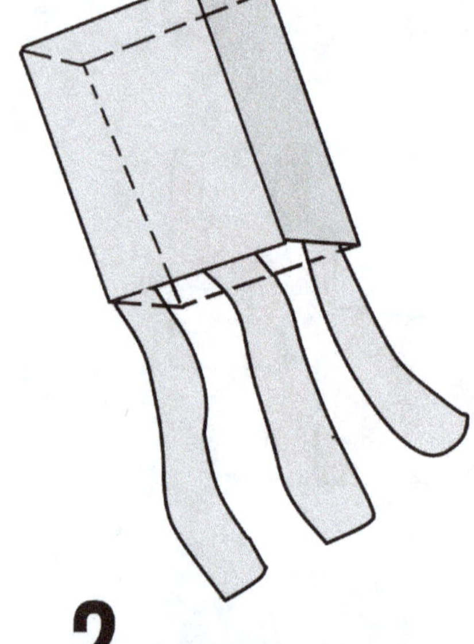

**2** NOW ADD A FEW TENTACLES

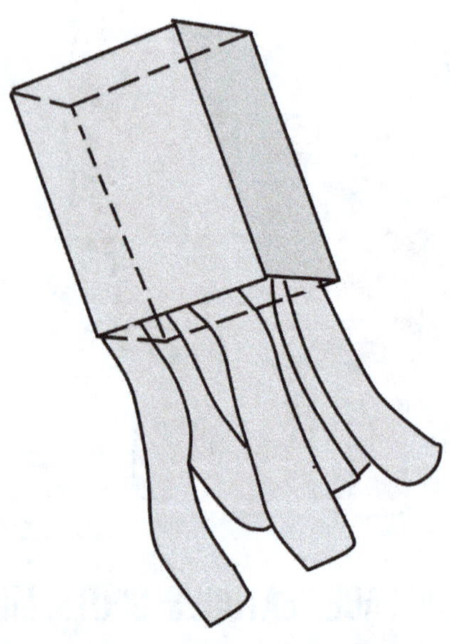

**3** ADD MORE TENTACLES AND ERASE DOTTED LINES

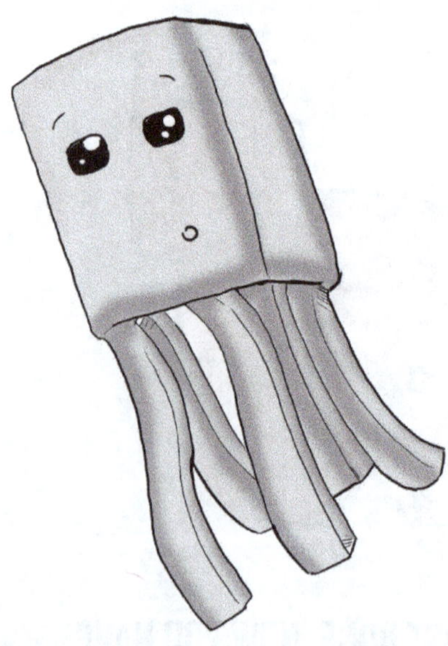

**4** ALMOST DONE, NOW YOU HAVE THE SHAPE OF THE SQUID, ADD ITS FACE FEATURES AND SOME SHADING AND THAT IS IT..

# SPIDER

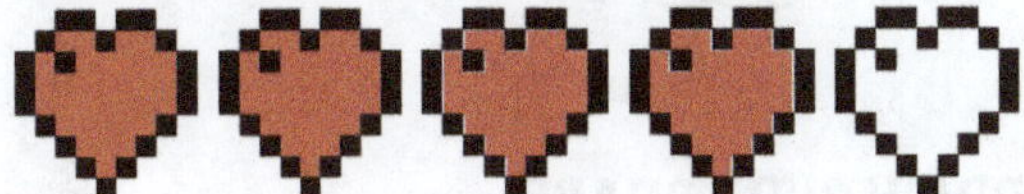

## DIFFICULTY LEVEL

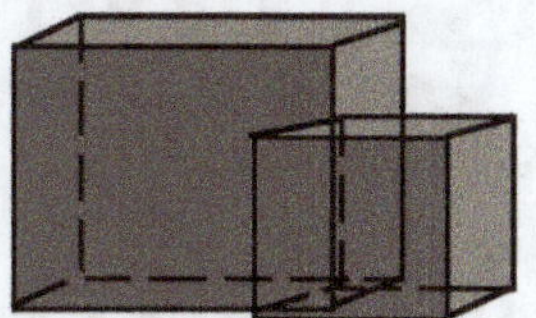

**1** START WITH A CUBOID. DRAW A SMALLER CUBE BESIDE IT AS SHOWN IN THE IMAGE.

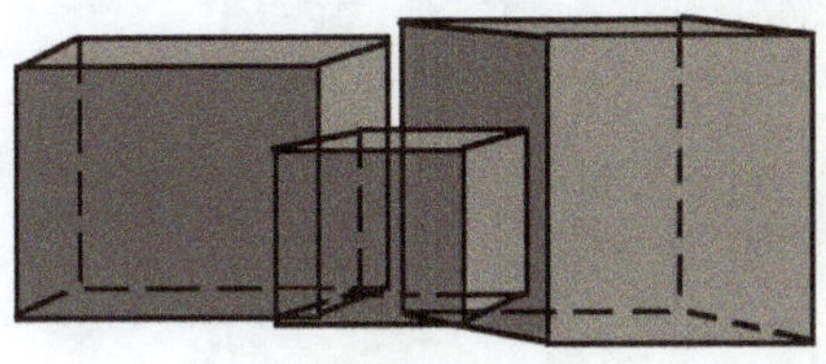

**2** NEXT DRAW ANOTHER BIGGER CUBE ON THE OTHER SIDE OF THE SMALLER CUBE TO COMPLETE THE SPIDER'S BODY.

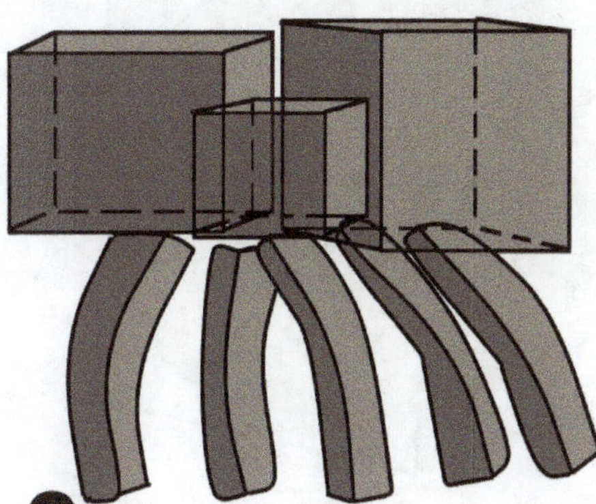

**3** ADD LEGS TO OUR SPIDER'S BODY AND ERASE DOTTED LINES.

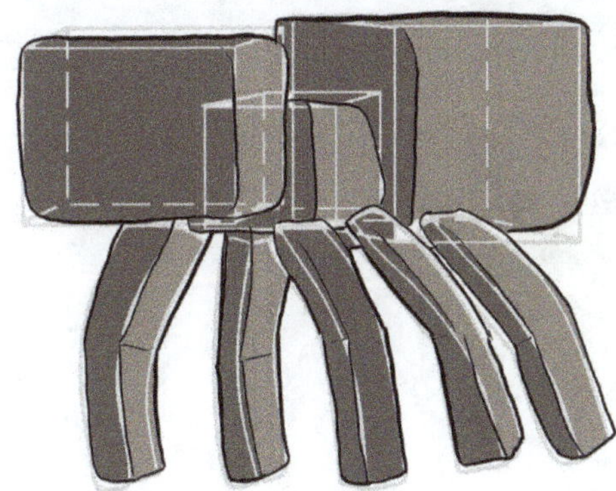

**4** ALMOST DONE, NOW YOU HAVE THE SHAPE OF THE SPIDER.

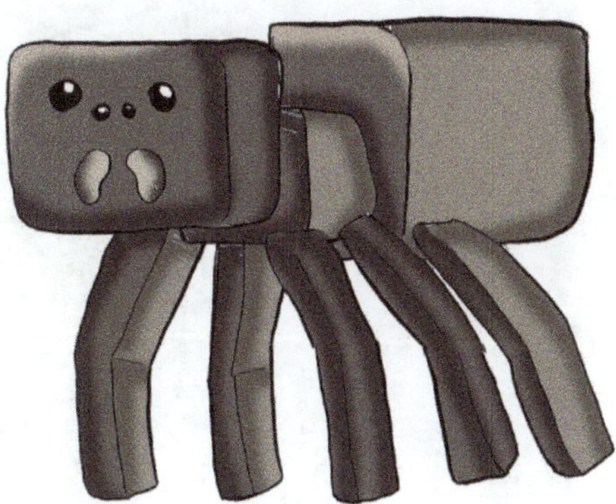

**5** ADD FACE FEATURES AND SOME SHADING AND YOU ARE DONE.

# SLIME

## DIFFICULTY LEVEL

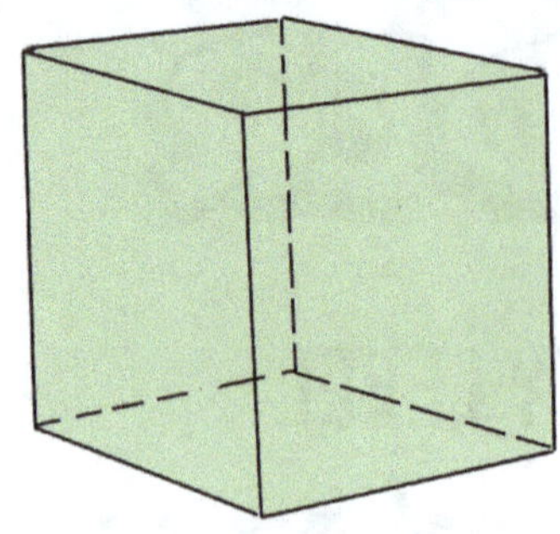

**1** FIRST DRAW CUBE SHAPE

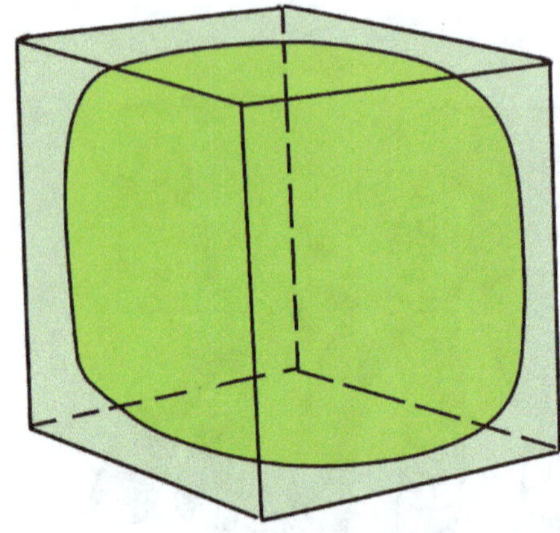

**2** NEXT DRAW THIS SHAPE WHITIN THE CUBE SHAPE

**3** ADD HIS FACE AND ERASE DOTTED LINES

**4** ALMOST DONE, NOW JUST ADD SOME FINAL DETAILS.

# ENDERMAN

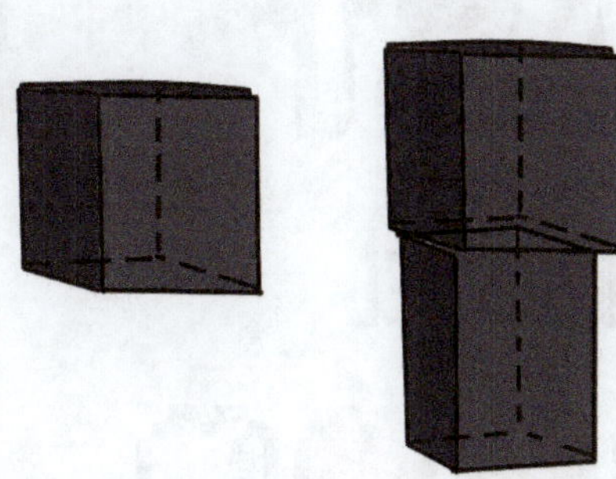

## DIFFICULTY LEVEL

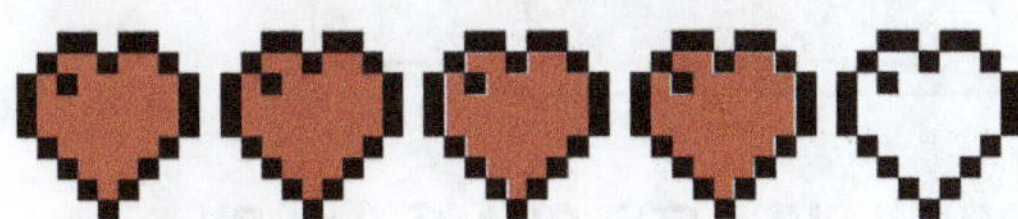

**1** FIRST DRAW CUBE FOR ENDERMAN'S HEAD AND ADD HIS TORSO.

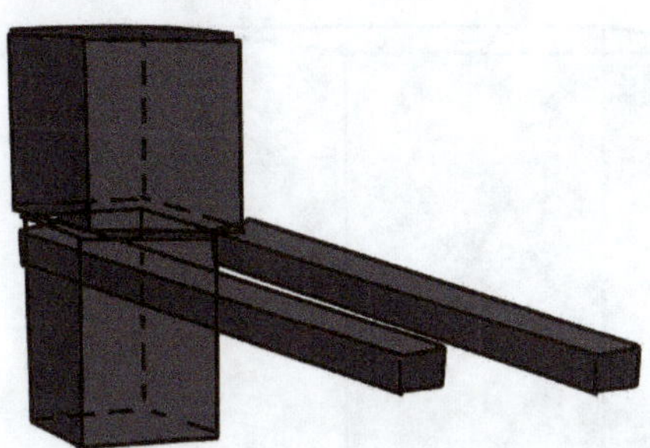

**2** NEXT DRAW HIS HANDS LIKE THIS.

**3** NOW DRAW HIS LEGS.

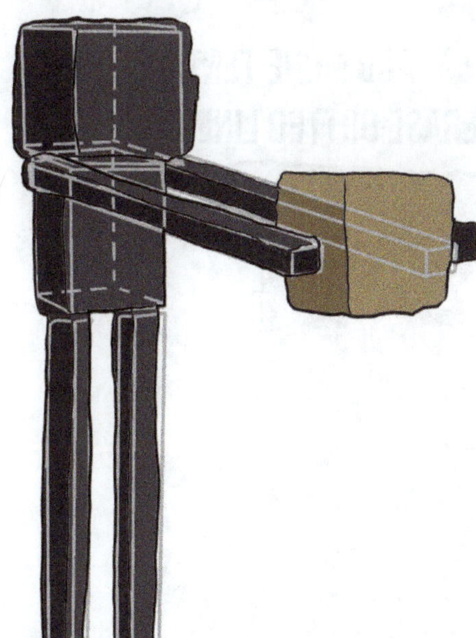

**4** ALMOST DONE, NOW YOU HAVE THE MAIN SHAPE OF THE ENDERMAN.

**5** ADD FACE FEATURES, SOME DETAILS, SOME SHADING AND YOU ARE DONE.

# GHAST

## DIFFICULTY LEVEL

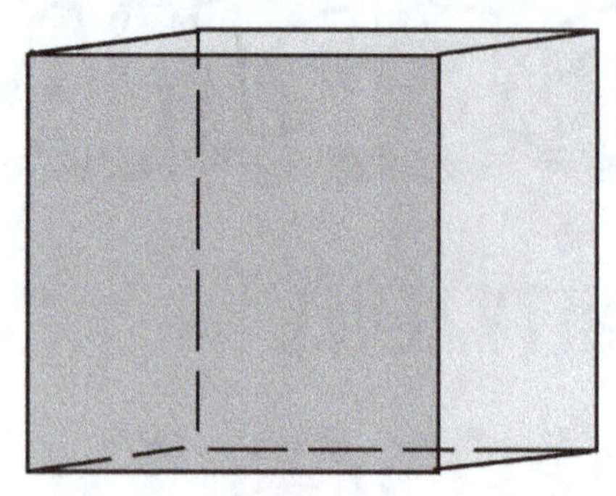

**1** FIRST DRAW CUBE FOR GHAST'S BODY

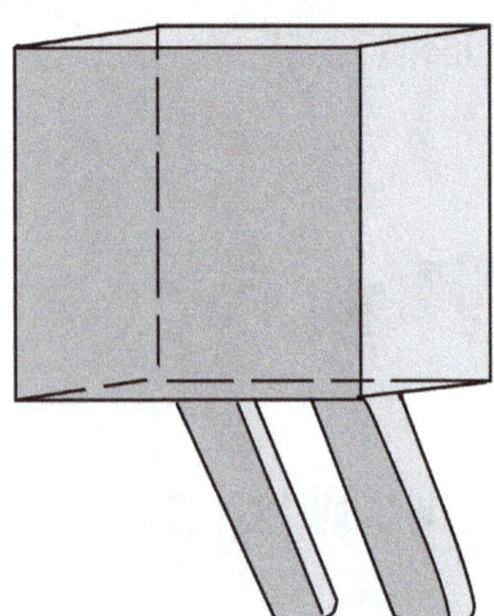

**2** NEXT DRAW A FEW TENTACLES

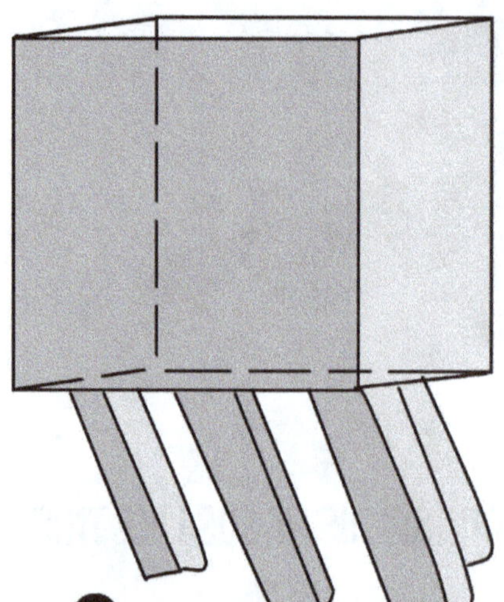

**3** ADD MORE TENTACLES AND ERASE DOTTED LINES

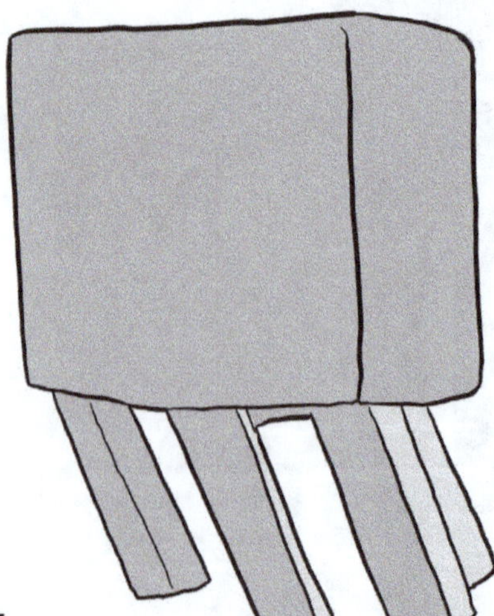

**4** . ALMOST DONE, NOW YOU HAVE THE SHAPE OF THE GHAST

**5** ADD FACE FEATURES, SOME DETAILS AND SOME SHADING AND YOU ARE DONE.

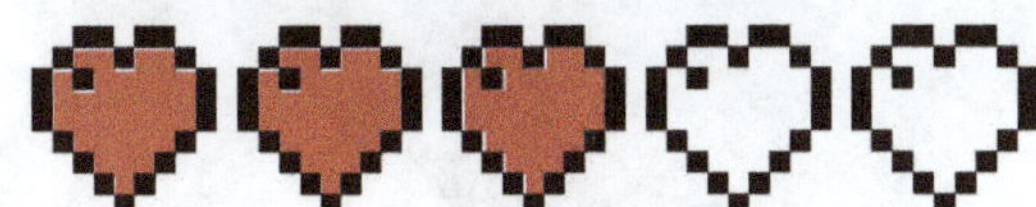

## DIFFICULTY LEVEL

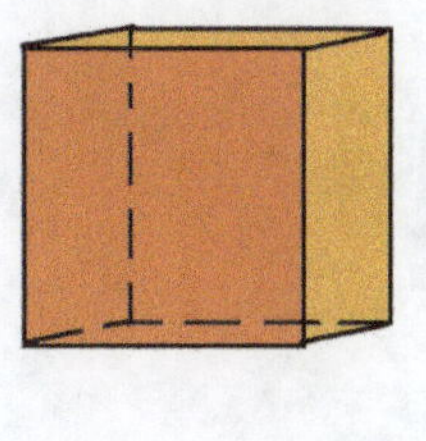
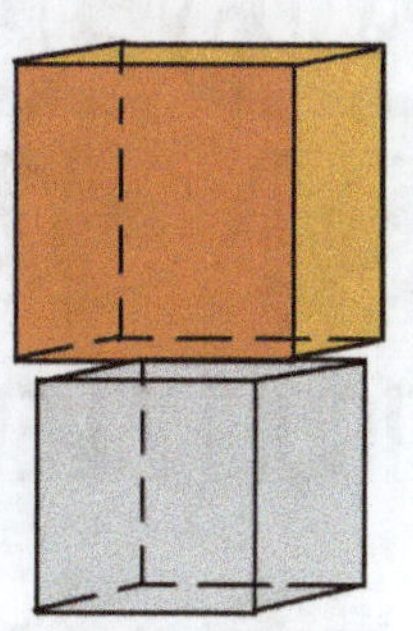

**1** FIRST DRAW CUBE FOR  HIS HEAD AND ANOTHER ONE FOR HIS TORSO.

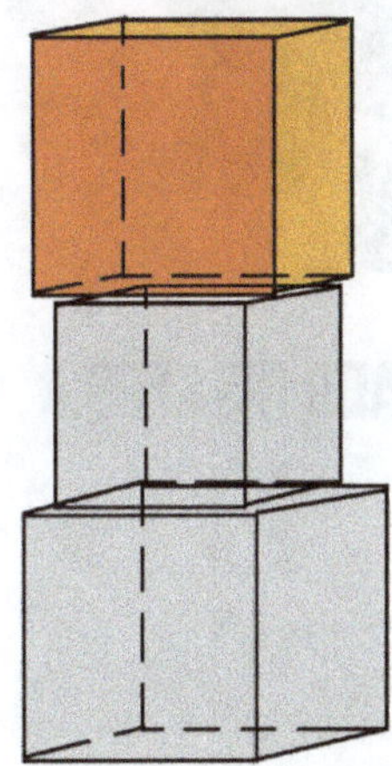

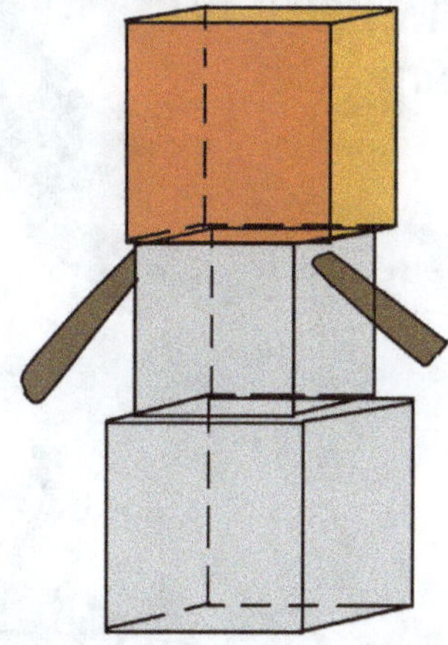

**2** NEXT DRAW ANOTHER CUBE TO GET HIS FULL BODY SHAPE .

**3** ADD HIS ARMS AND ERASE DOTTED LINES.

**4** ALMOST DONE, NOW DRAW HIS FACE.

**5** ADD MORE DETAILS AND SOME SHADING AND YOU ARE DONE.

# ENDER DRAGON

## DIFFICULTY LEVEL

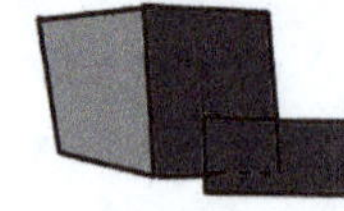

**1** FIRST DRAW A CUBE FOR HIS HEAD AND ADD HIS EARS AND SNOUT.

**2** NEXT DRAW TORSO, NECK AND TAIL LIKE THIS.

**3** NEXT, ADD HIS LEGS.

**4** ALMOST DONE, NOW DRAW HIS WINGS FOLLOWING THIS

**5** ADD FACE FEATURES, ERASE DOTTED LINES AND YOU HAVE MAIN SHAPE OF OUR DRAGON.

**6** ADD SOME MORE DETAILS AND SOME SHADING AND YOU ARE DONE.

# BOW AND ARROW

## DIFFICULTY LEVEL

**1** FIRST DRAW MAIN SHAPE OF BOW AND LINE FOR ARROW.

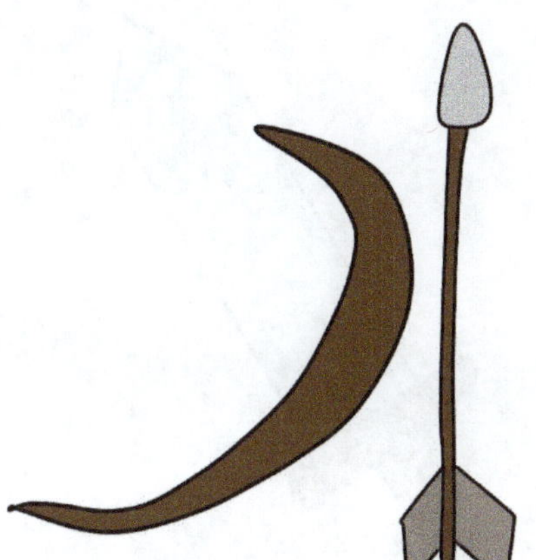

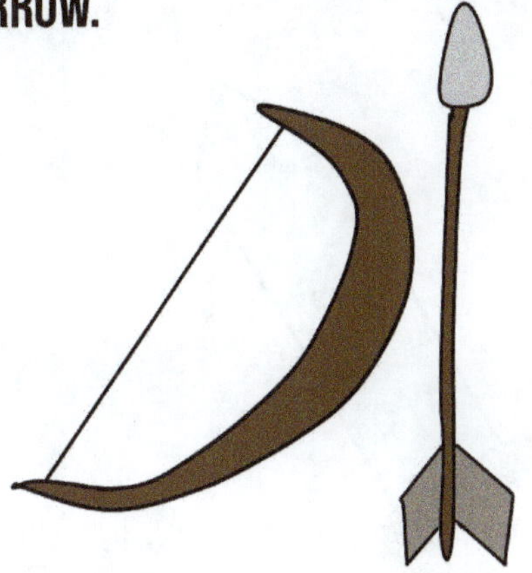

**2** NEXT DRAW THESE SHAPES FOR ARROW.

**3** ADD A LINE FOR BOW'S STRING.

**4** ALMOST DONE, NOW DRAW SOME DETAILS.

**5** ADD FEW DETAILS AND SOME SHADING AND YOU ARE DONE.

# SWORD

## DIFFICULTY LEVEL

**1** FIRST DRAW THIS SHAPE FOR BLADE

**2** NEXT DRAW THIS SHAPE

**3** NEXT ADD THIS SHAPE FOR HANDLE

**4** . ALMOST DONE, NOW YOU HAVE THE MAIN SHAPE OF THE SWORD.

**5** ADD SOME DETAILS AND SHADING LINES AND YOU ARE DONE.

# CREEPER

## DIFFICULTY LEVEL

**1** FIRST DRAW THE SHAPE OF A CREEPER'S HEAD.

**2** DRAW A RECTANGULAR CUBOID BELOW HIS HEAD TO CREATE HIS TORSO.

**3** NEXT DRAW HIS LEGS.

**4** ALMOST DONE! NOW WHEN YOU HAVE THE SHAPE OF THE CREEPER USE THICKER LINES TO DRAW HIS FINAL SHAPE.

**5** FEW MORE DETAILS AND OUR CREEPER IS DONE! ADD HIM A FACE, SOME SPOTS AND HE IS DONE.

# AXE

## DIFFICULTY LEVEL

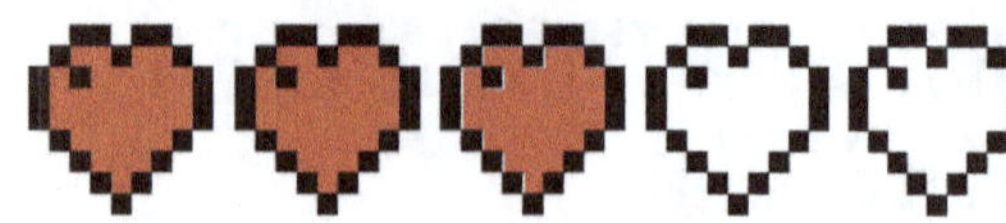

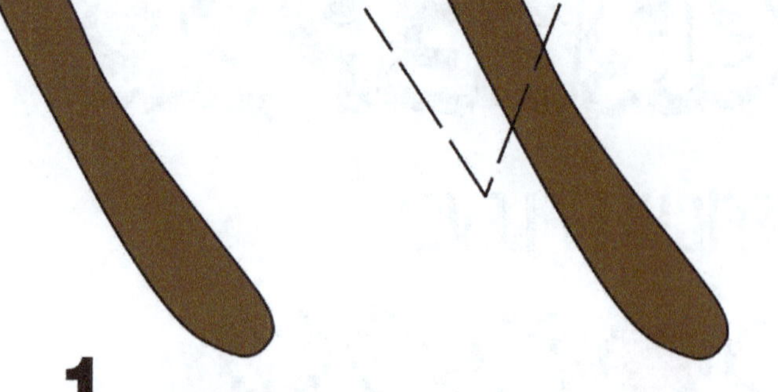

**1** FIRST DRAW THIS SHAPE FOR AXE'S HANDLE AND DRAW A TRIANGLE.

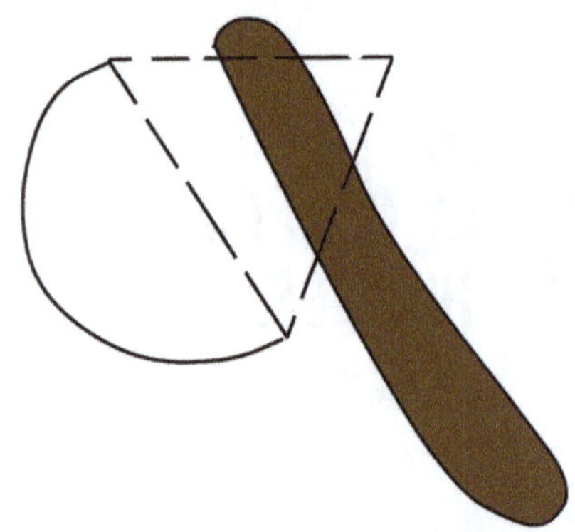

**2** NEXT DRAW THIS SHAPE TO HAVE THE BLADE PART OF THE AXE.

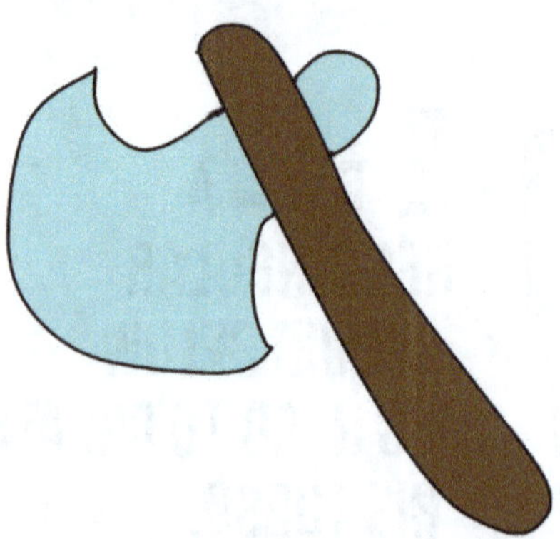

**3** FOLLOW THE SHAPE ABOVE AND REMOVE THE EXCESS LINES.

**4** ALMOST DONE, NOW YOU HAVE MAIN SHAPE OF AXE

**5** ADD SOME DETAILS, LINES AND SOME SHADING AND YOU ARE DONE.

# GUARDIAN

## DIFFICULTY LEVEL

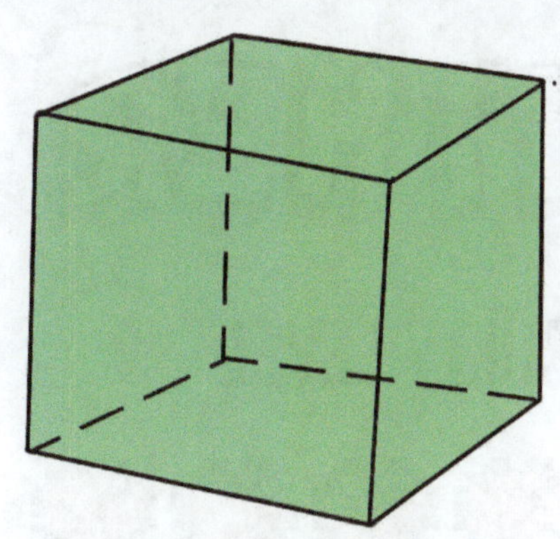

**1** FIRST DRAW CUBE FOR GUARDIAN'S HEAD.

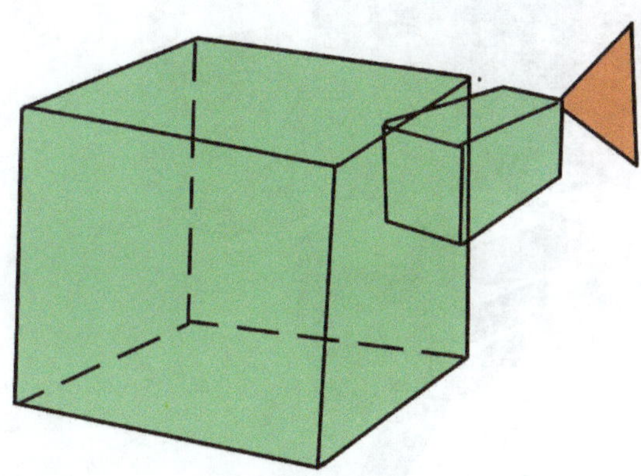

**2** NEXT DRAW THESE SHAPES FOR HIS TAIL AND FIN

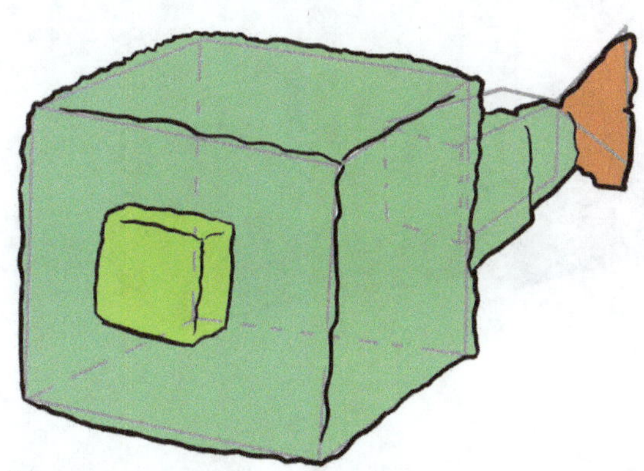

**3** ADD A SMALL CUBE FOR HIS EYE

**4** ALMOST DONE, NOW DRAW FEW MORE CUBE SHAPES FOR BUMPS ON HIS BODY

**5** ADD DETAILS FOR HIS EYE, SOME LINES, SOME SHADING AND THAT IS IT

# WITHER

## DIFFICULTY LEVEL

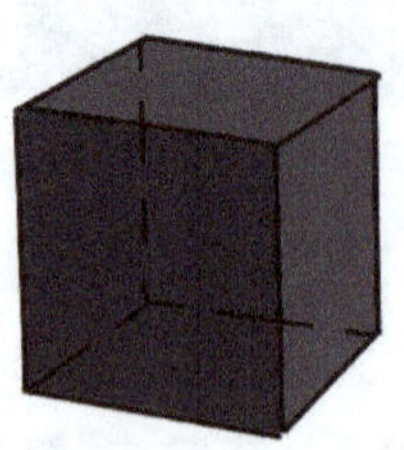

**1** FIRST DRAW CUBE FOR WITHER'S HEAD.

**2** ADD TWO MORE CUBES

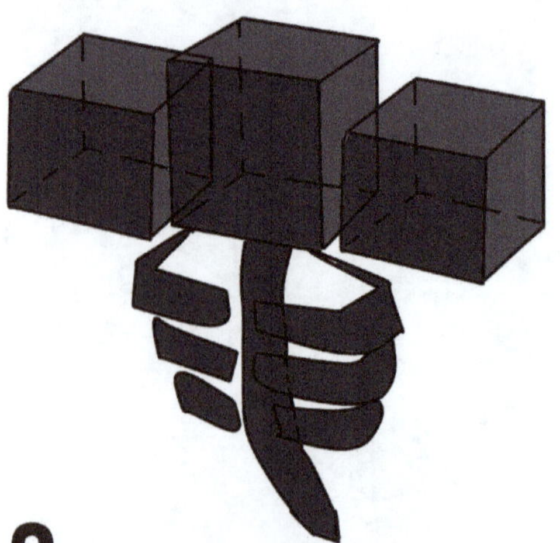

**3** NEXT DRAW LINES FOR HIS BODY TO GET THIS SHAPE LIKE THIS

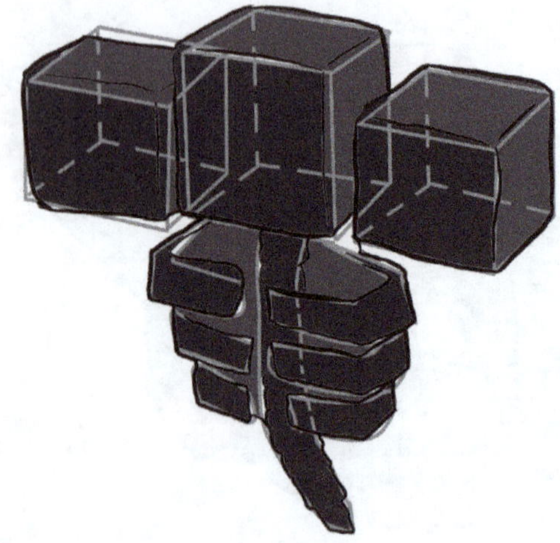

**4** ALMOST DONE! NOW YOU HAVE THE MAIN SHAPE OF THE WITHER. ERASE DOTTED LINES.

**5** ADD FACE FEATURES, SOME DETAILS SOME SHADING AND OUR WITHER IS DONE.

# IRON GOLEM

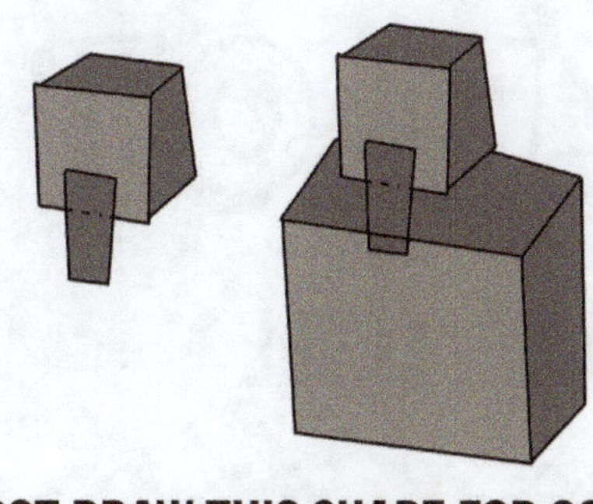

## DIFFICULTY LEVEL

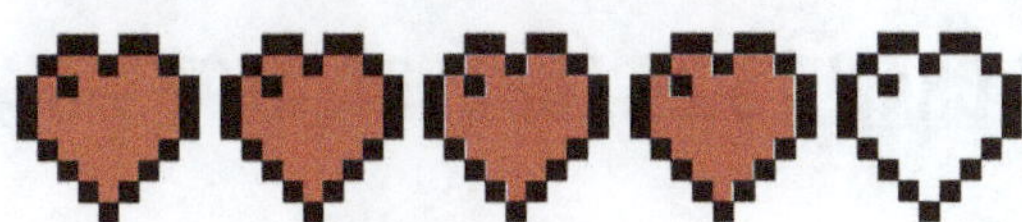

**1** . FIRST DRAW THIS SHAPE FOR GOLEM'S HEAD AND DRAW HIS TORSO.

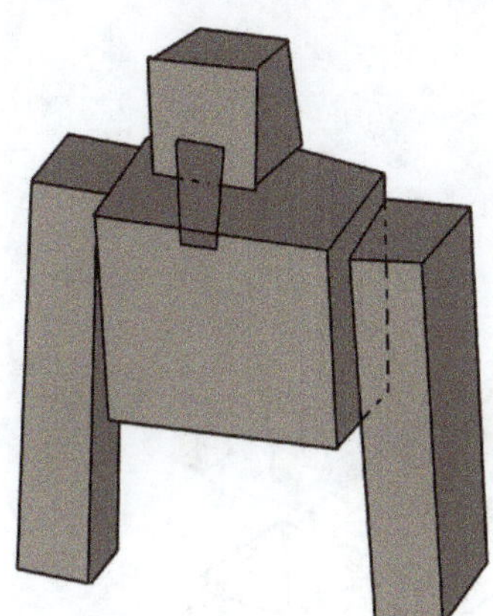

**2** ADD HIS ARMS AS SHOWN I N THE IMAGE.

**3** THEN ADD LOWER PART OF HIS BODY AND LEGS.

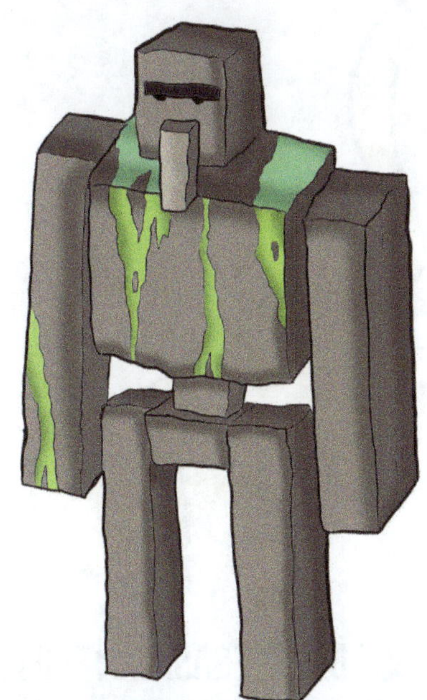

**4** ALMOST DONE, DRAW HIS FACE AND ERASE DOTTED LINES AND NOW YOU HAVE THE SHAPE OF THE GOLEM.

**5** ADD SOME LINES FOR TEXTURE AND SOME SHADING AND THAT IS IT..

# OCELOT

## DIFFICULTY LEVEL

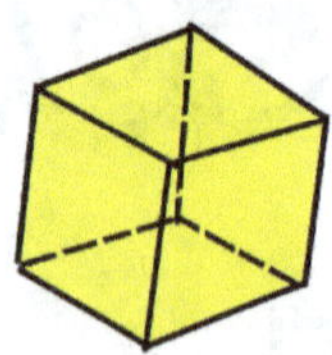

**1** FIRST, DRAW A CUBE FOR THE OCELOT'S HEAD.

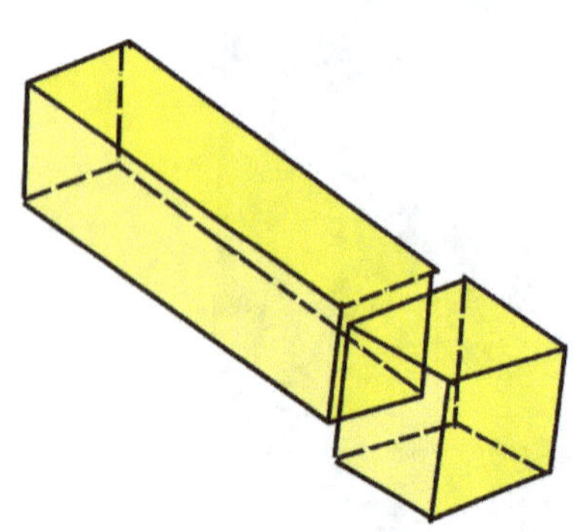

**2** NEXT DRAW THIS SHAPE FOR ITS TORSO

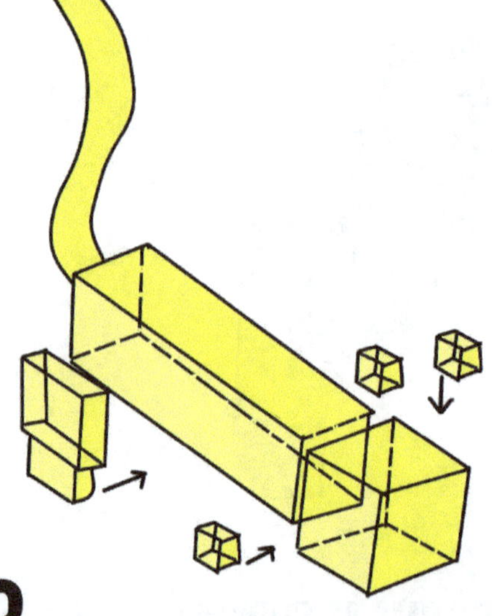

**3** ADD LEGS, EARS AND OCELOT'S TAIL.

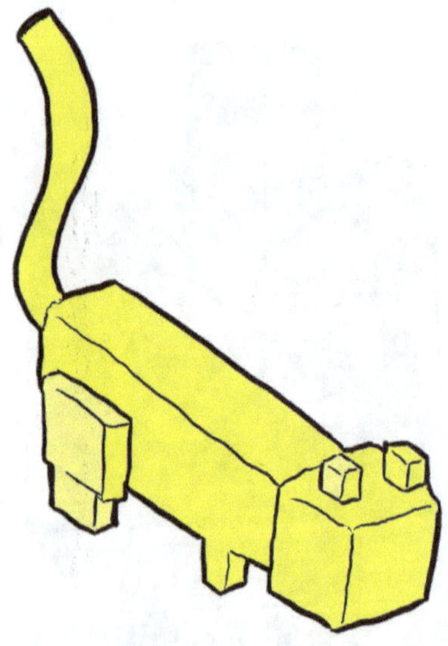

**4** ALMOST DONE, ERASE DOTTED LINES AND NOW WE HAVE MAIN SHAPE OF OCELOT

**5** ADD FACE FEATURES, LINES AND SOME SHADING AND YOU ARE DONE.

# LLAMA

## DIFFICULTY LEVEL

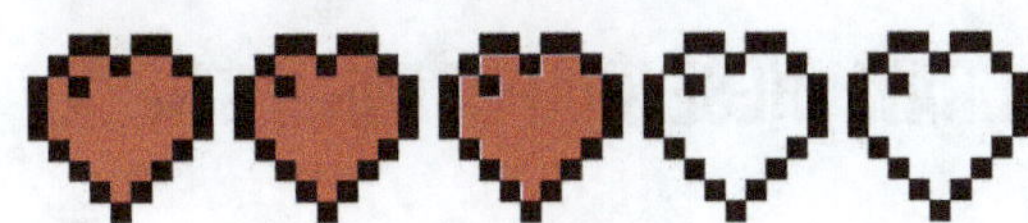

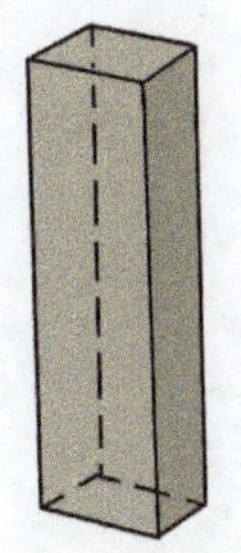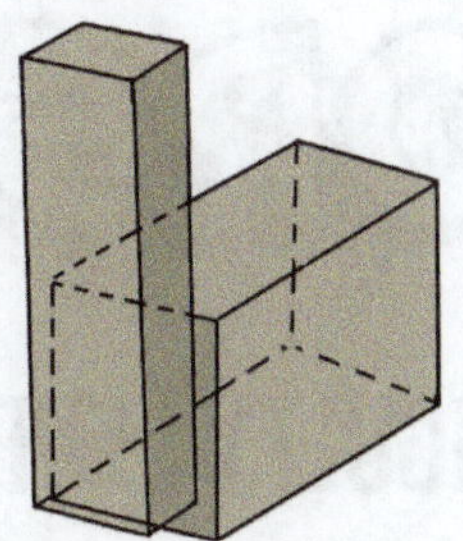

**1** FIRST DRAW THE SHAPE OF THE LLAMA'S BODY.

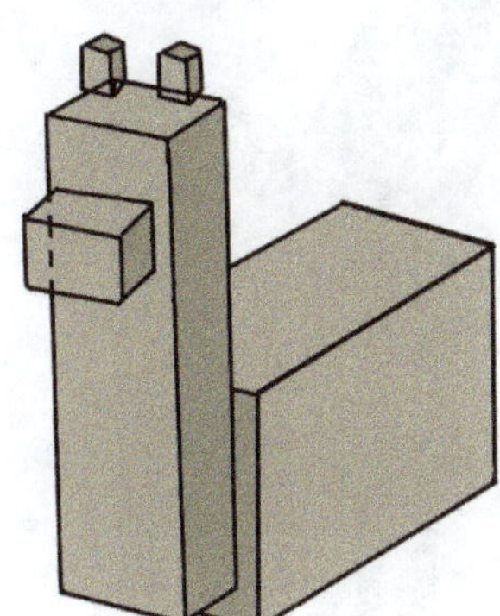

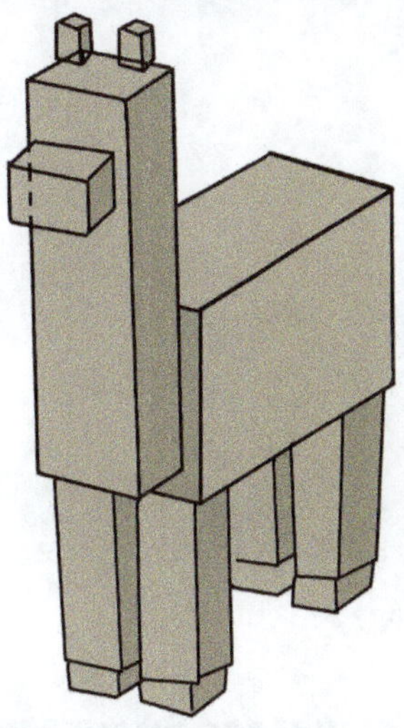

**2** NEXT ERASE DOTTED LINES AND ADD EARS AND SNOUT

**3** NOW ADD LLAMA'S LEGS.

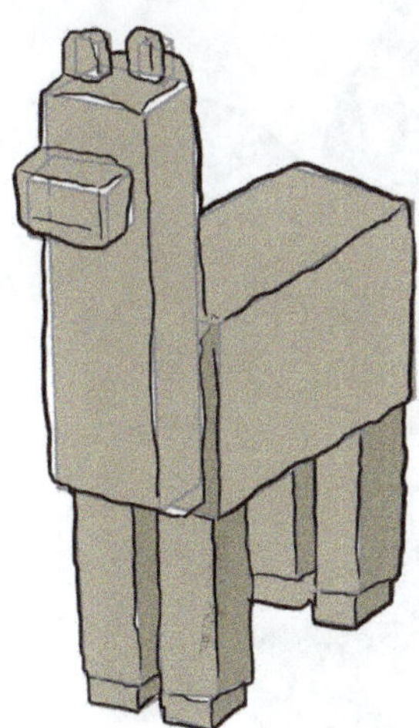

**4** ALMOST DONE, NOW YOU HAVE THE SHAPE OF THE LLAMA,

**5** ADD FACE FEATURES, ITS SADDLE AND SOME SHADING AND YOU ARE DONE.

# HORSE

## DIFFICULTY LEVEL

**1** FIRST DRAW THESE SHAPES FOR HIS NECK AND BODY.

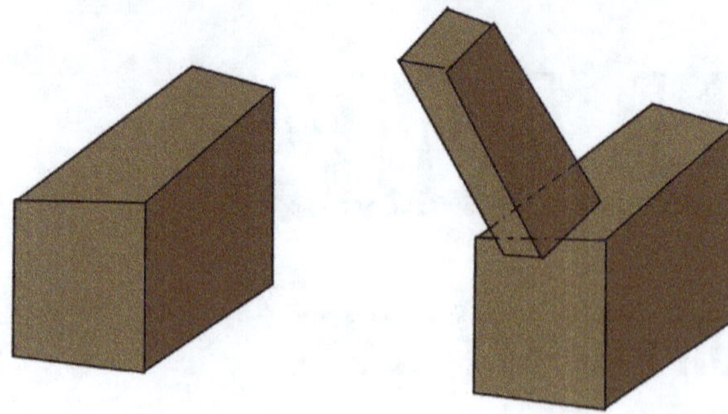

**2** NEXT DRAW FEW MORE SHAPES FOR HORSE'S SNOUT AND MANE.

**3** ADD LEGS AND HORSE'S TAIL

**4** ALMOST DONE, NOW YOU HAVE THE SHAPE OF THE HORSE AND ERASE DOTTED LINES.

**5** ADD FACE FEATURES, ITS SADDLE AND SOME SHADING AND YOU ARE DONE.

# LILAC

## DIFFICULTY LEVEL

**1** FIRST DRAW STEM OF LILAC.

**2** ADD FLOWERS TO OUR PLANT.

**3** ALMOST DONE, NOW ADD SOME LEAVES.

**4** ADD FEW MORE DETAILS TO BRING OUR PLANT TO LIFE AND THAT IS IT.

# SKELETON

## DIFFICULTY LEVEL

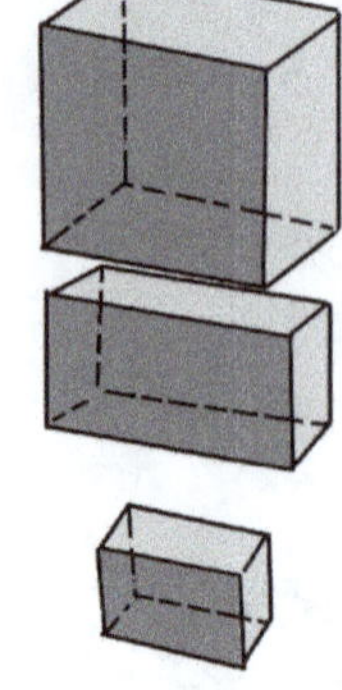

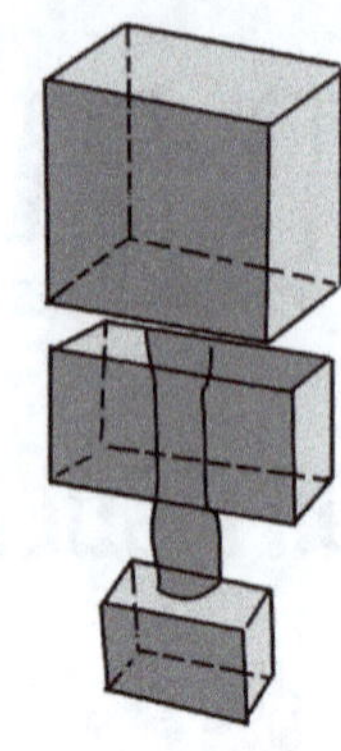

**1** FIRST DRAW CUBIC SHAPES FOR HIS HEAD AND BODY

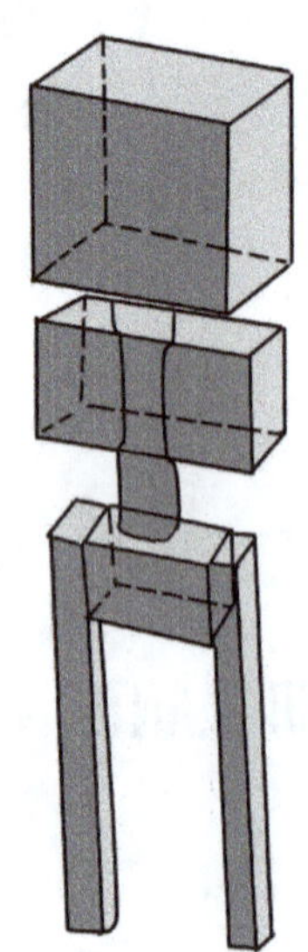

**2** DRAW HIS LEGS.

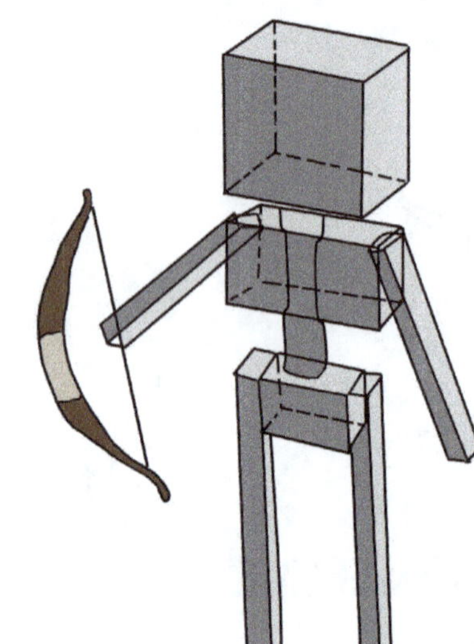

**3** NEXT STEP IS TO ADD HIS HANDS AND A BOW ERASE DOTTED LINES

**4** ALMOST DONE! NOW WHEN YOU HAVE A SHAPE OF SKELETON'S BODY USE THICKER LINES TO DRAW HIS FINAL SHAPE.

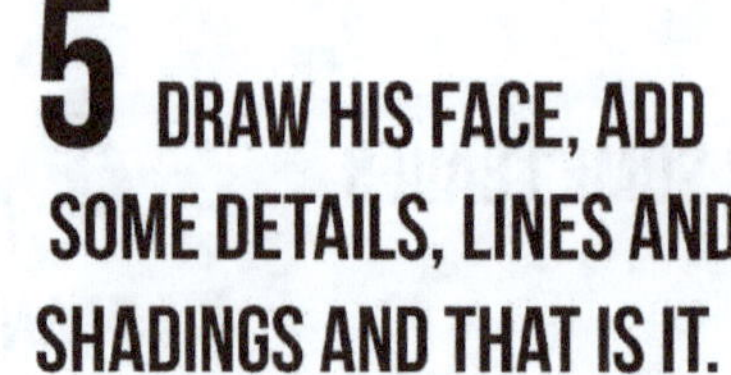

**5** DRAW HIS FACE, ADD SOME DETAILS, LINES AND SHADINGS AND THAT IS IT.

# VILLAGER

## DIFFICULTY LEVEL

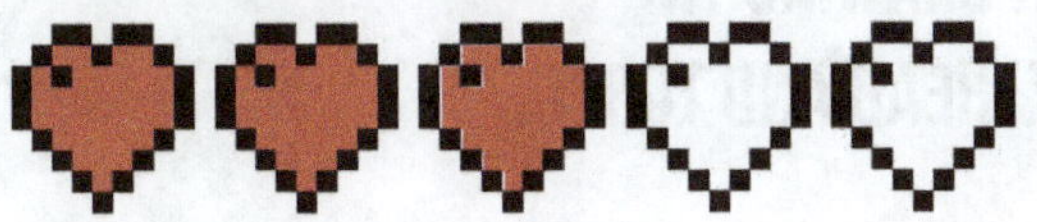

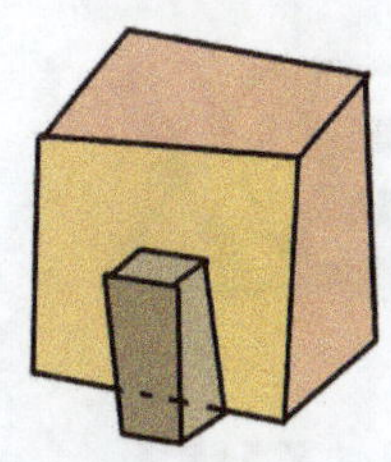

**1** FIRST DRAW THE SHAPE OF A VILLAGER'S HEAD.

**2** ADD HIS ARMS.

**3** NEXT STEP IS EASY. JUST FOLLOW OUR LEAD AND DRAW HIS TORSO

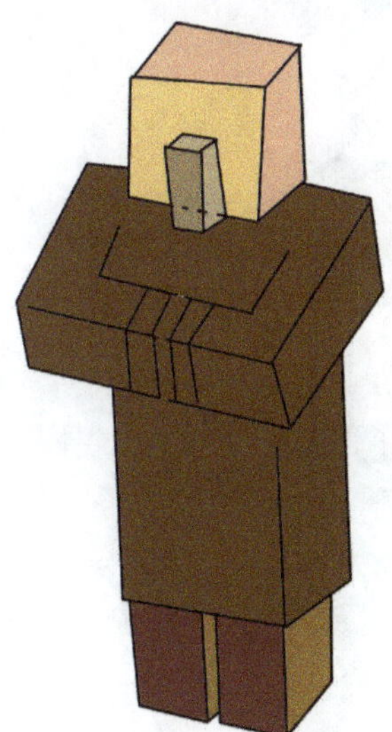

**4** NOW JUST ADD HIS LEGS

**5** ALMOST DONE. NOW DRAW HIS FACE FEATURES

**6** FEW MORE DETAILS AND SOME SHADING AND OUR VILLAGER IS DONE.

# ALEX

## DIFFICULTY LEVEL

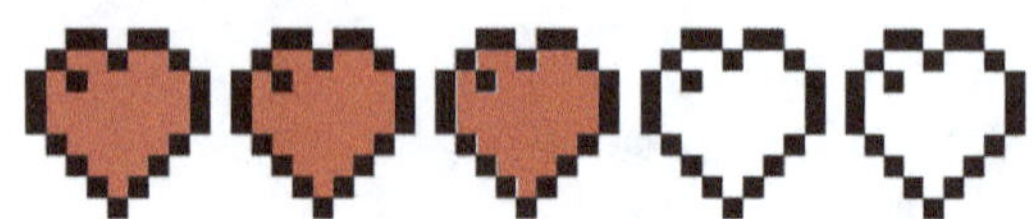

**1** START WITH DRAWING THE SHAPE OF ALEX' HEAD AND TORSO.

**2** DRAW HER HANDS. ERASE DOTTED LINES.

**3** NEXT STEP IS EASY. JUST FOLLOW OUR LEAD AND DRAW HER LEGS.

**4** ALMOST DONE! NOW WHEN YOU HAVE THE SHAPE OF ALEX USE THICKER LINES TO DRAW HER FINAL SHAPE.

# CHEST

## DIFFICULTY LEVEL

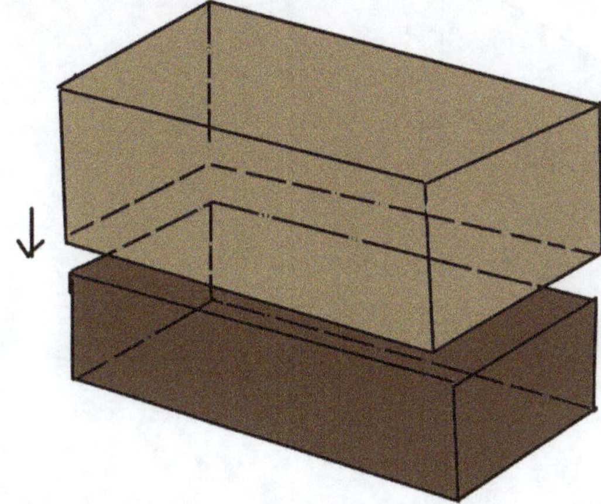

**1** DRAW TWO CUBOID AS SHOWN

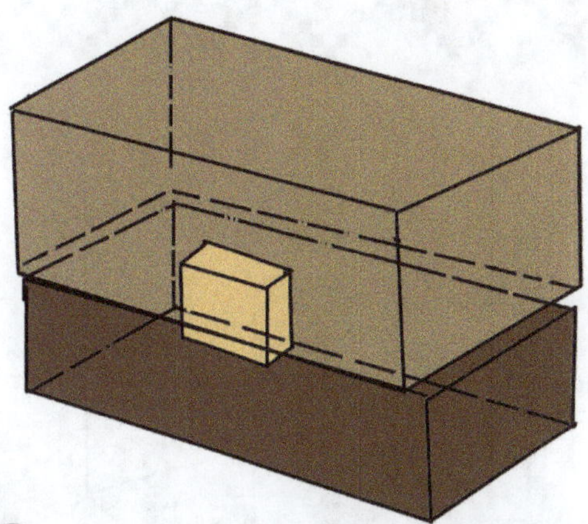

**2** NOW DRAW A SMALL CUBOID FOR KEY HOLE. ERASE DOTTED LINES.

**3** ALMOST DONE, NOW WE HAVE SHAPE OF CHEST

**4** TO FINISH ADD SOME DETAILS AND SOME SHADING AND THAT IS IT.

# FURNACE

## DIFFICULTY LEVEL

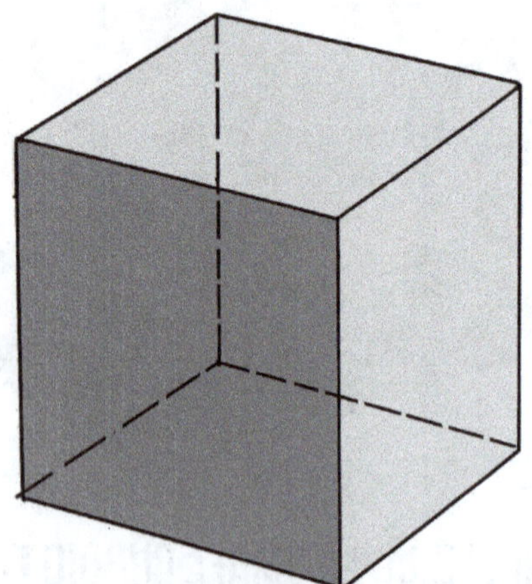

**1** DRAW A CUBE LIKE THIS.

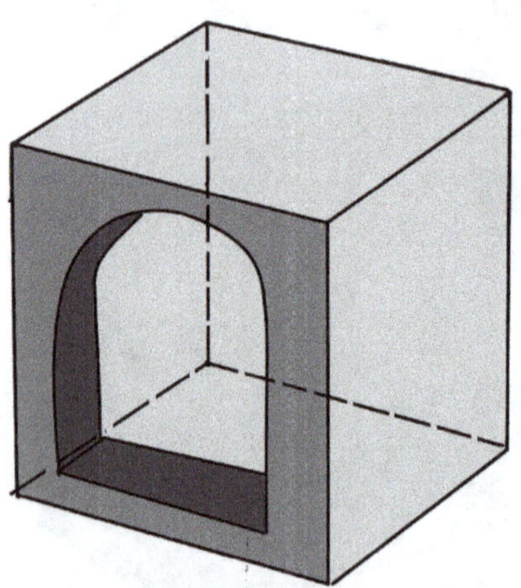

**2** NOW DRAW SHAPE LIKE THIS ONE FOR FIRE HOLE, ERASE DOTTED LINES.

**3** ALMOST DONE, NOW ADD SOME FLAMES INSIDE OUR SHAPE.

**4** ADD SOME SHAPES FOR STONES, AND SOME MORE DETAILS LIKE THIS AND YOU ARE DONE.

# ANVIL

## DIFFICULTY LEVEL

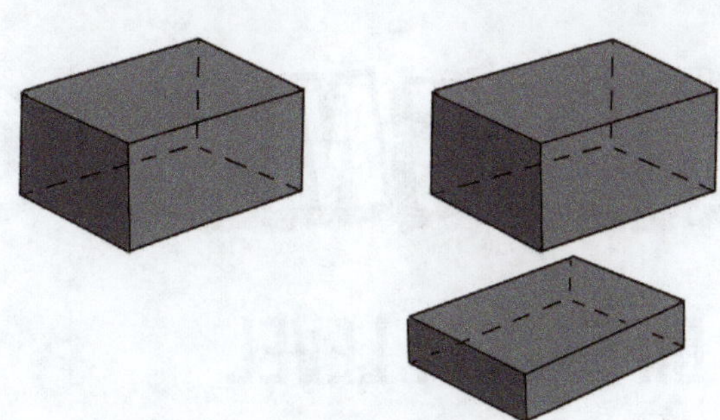

**1** FIRST DRAW CUBOIDS LIKE THIS.

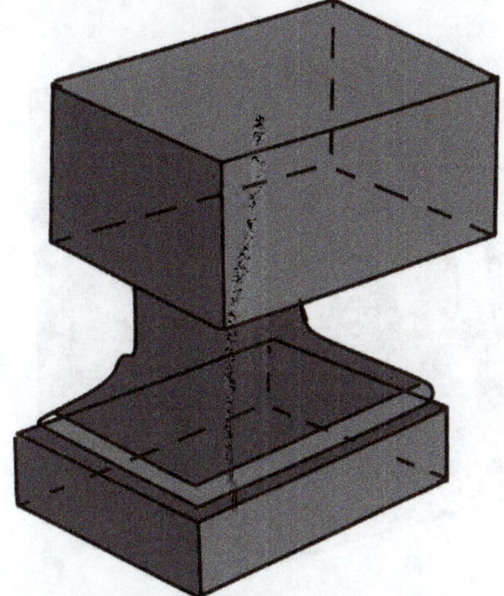

**2** NEXT CONNECT THE TWO CUBOIDS AS SHOWN.

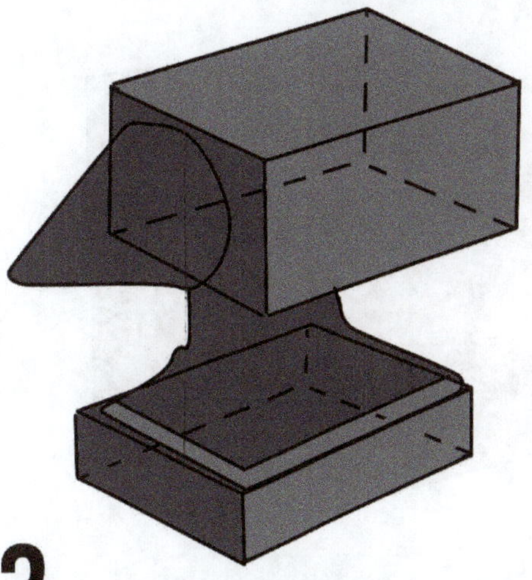

**3** DRAW A CONE SHAPE ON THE UPPER CUBOID.

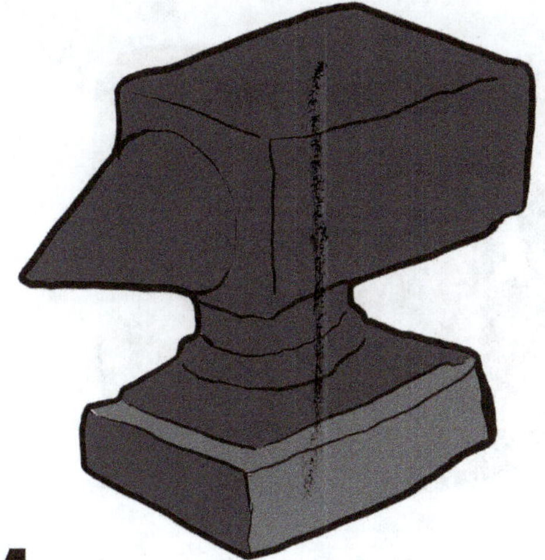

**4** ALMOST DONE NOW YOU HAVE THE SHAPE OF THE ANVIL.

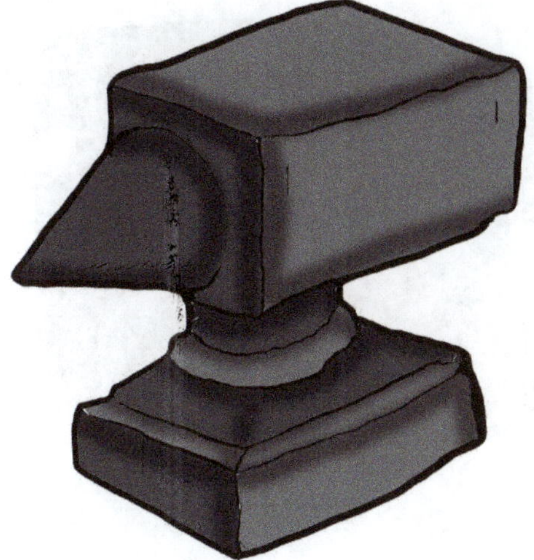

**5** ADD SOME MORE LINES, SHADINGS AND DETAILS ON YOUR ANVIL TO FINISH THE DRAWING.

# MAGMA CUBE

**DIFFICULTY LEVEL**

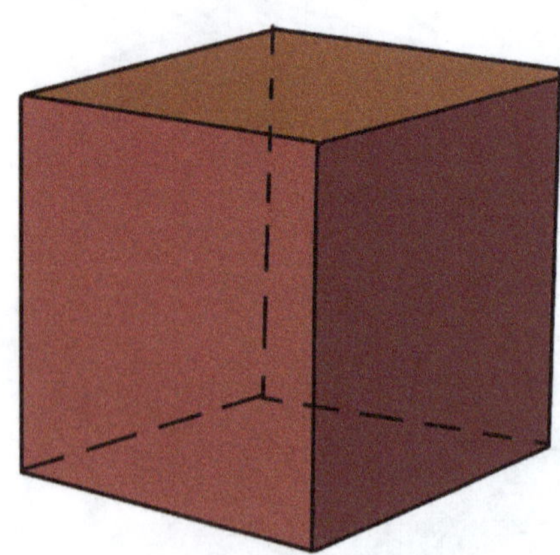

**1** DRAW A CUBE.

**2** NOW DRAW ITS EYES LIKE THIS.

**3** MAKE EDGES SOFTER LIKE THIS AND ERASE DOTTED LINES.

**4** ALMOST DONE, JUST ADD SOME ROUND SHAPES FOR DETAILS AND YOU ARE DONE.

# SUNFLOWER

DIFFICULTY LEVEL

**1** DRAW STEM AND SHAPE OF OUR SUNFLOWER.

**2** NOW DRAW ITS LEAVES ON STEM.

**3** ALMOST DONE NOW ADD SOME SMALLER PETALS IN THE CENTER OF FLOWER.

**4** ADD FEW MORE DETALIS AND OUR SUNFLOWER IS DONE.

# PICKAXE

## DIFFICULTY LEVEL

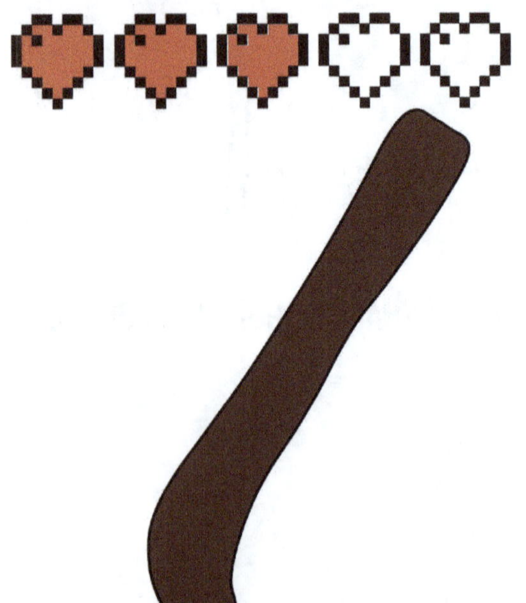

**1** DRAW HANDLE SHAPE

**2** NEXT DRAW THIS SHAPE FOR TOP PART OF OUR PICKAXE

**3** ALMOST DONE, ADD SOME LINES FOR ROPE

**4** ADD SOME MORE LINES AND DETAILS ON THE HANDLE PART FOR WOOD TEXTURE AND WE ARE DONE.

# ARMOR STAND

## DIFFICULTY LEVEL

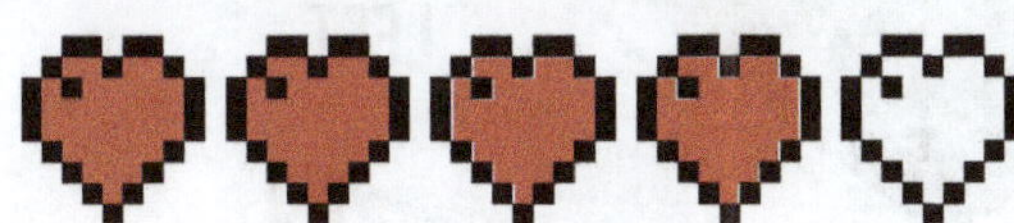

**1** DRAW THE SHAPE OF AN ARMOR.

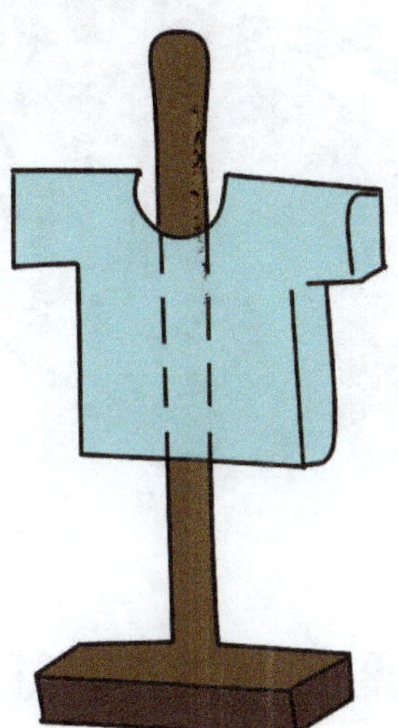

**2** DRAW A STAND FOLLOWING THE IMAGE ABOVE.

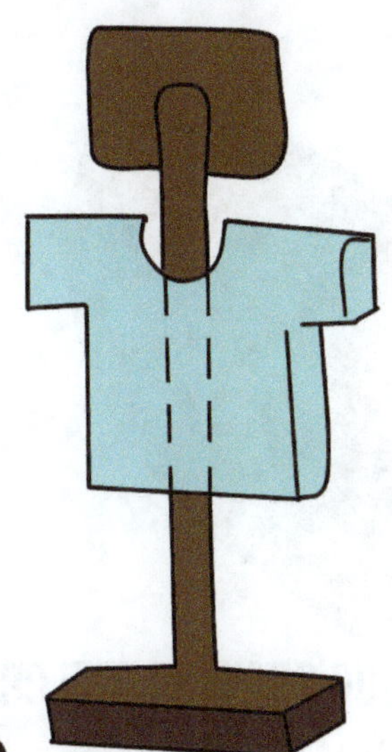

**3** NOW DRAW A HELMET.

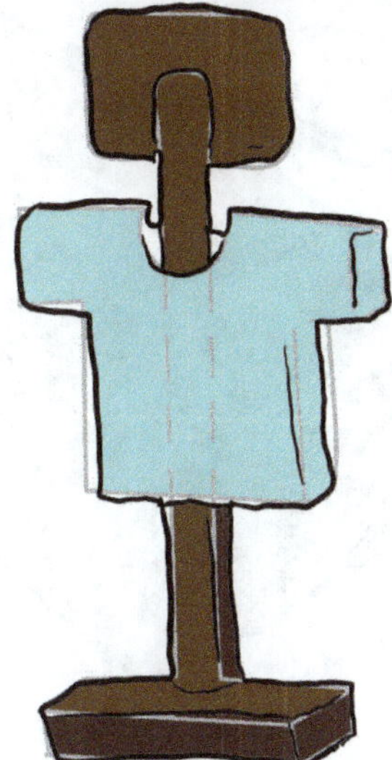

**4** FOLLOW LINE GUIDES AND TRACE THE FINAL SHAPE. ERASE ALL LINE GUIDES.

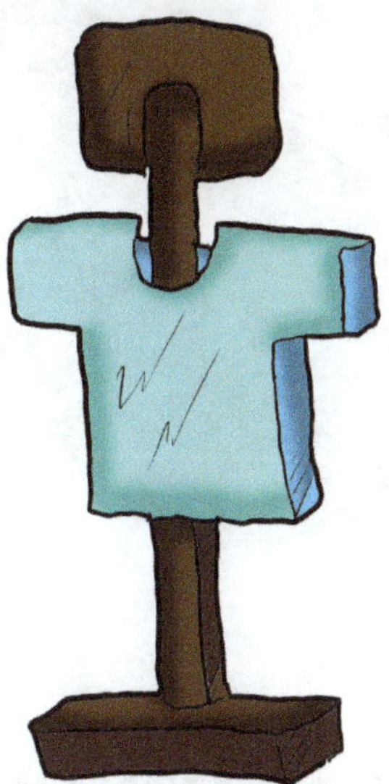

**5** TO MAKE IT MORE REALISTIC, USE THIN LINES FOR SMALL DETAILS AND SHADING.

# BOAT



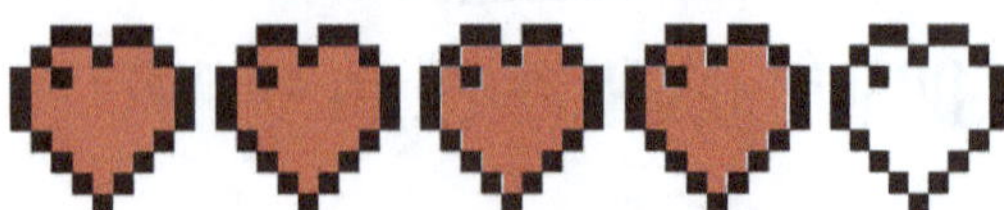

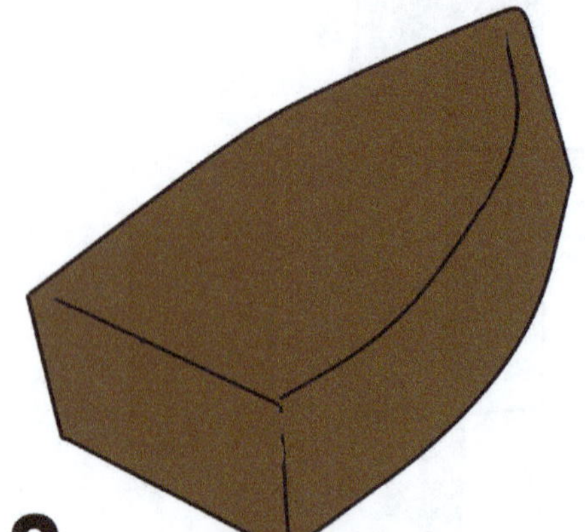

**2** FOLLOW OUR DRAWING AND DRAW A SHAPE OF A BOAT.

**3** NOW, DRAW THE BOTTOM PART OF THE BOAT AND 2 PADDLES.

**4** FOLLOW THE LINE GUIDES AND TRACE THE FINAL SHAPE OF THE BOAT AND DRAW THE BOAT'S SITTING BENCH.

**5** USE SHADINGS AND THIN LINES TO FINISH YOUR DRAWING.

# COMPASS



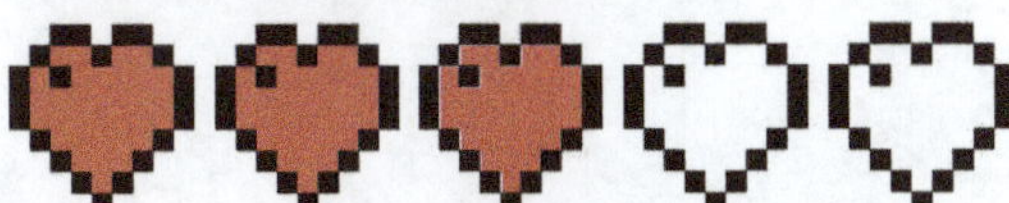

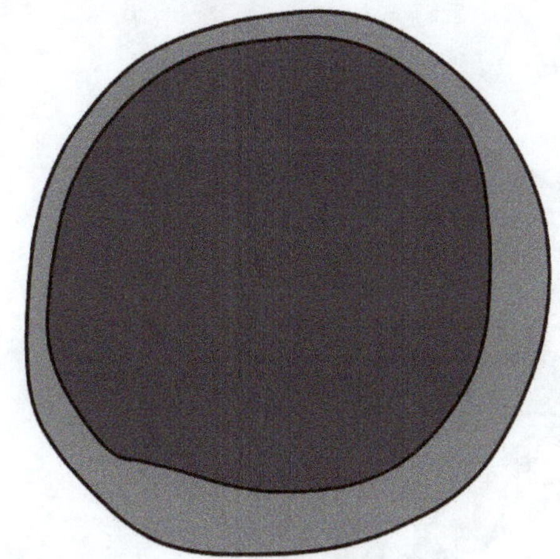

**1** DRAW TWO CIRCLES, ONE INSIDE ANOTHER.

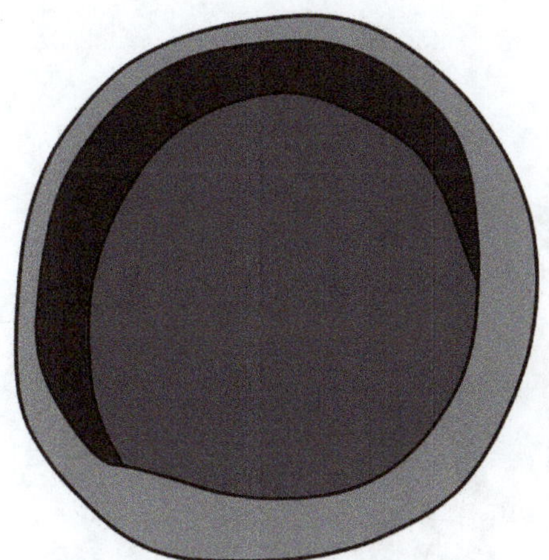

**2** FORM A MOON-LIKE SHAPE INSIDE FIRST CIRCLE.

**3** USE LINE GUIDES TO TRACE THE SHAPE OF THE COMPASS. DRAW THE NEEDLE OF THE COMPASS.

**4** TO FINISH IT, DRAW SOME DETAILS AND ADD GLASS REFLECTION ON THE COMPASS.

# DIFFICULTY LEVEL

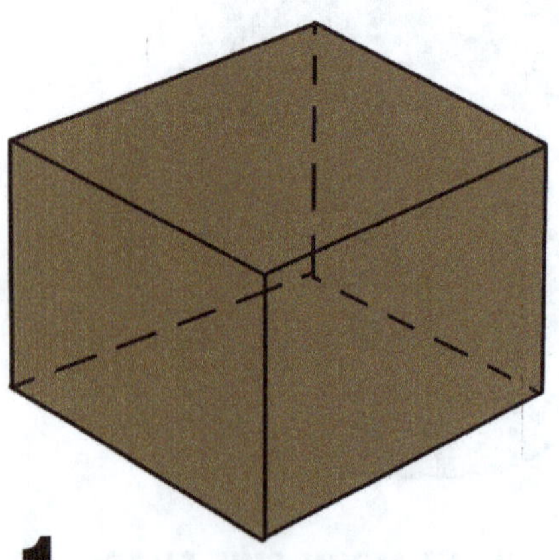

**1** START WITH A CUBE.

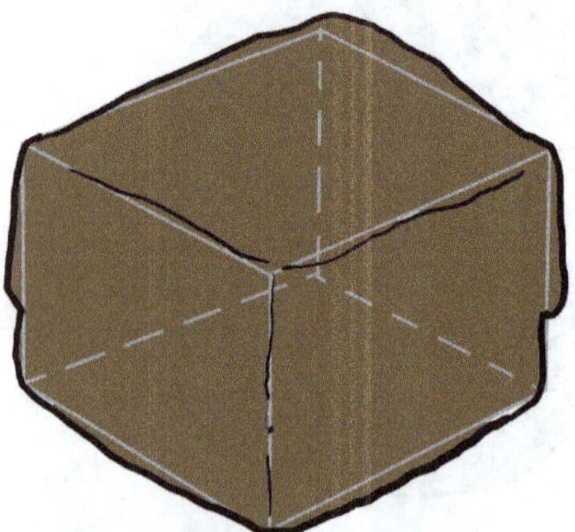

**2** TRACE A SHAPE OF A CAKE.

**3** ERASE GUIDELINES AND DRAW A CREAM.

**4** ALMOST DONE! DRAW SOME FROSTING AND SMALL DETAILS, AND YOUR CAKE IS DONE!

**1** START WITH DRAWING THE SHAPE OF THE BAT'S HEAD AND TORSO.

**2** THEN DRAW HIS WINGS AND EARS. ERASE DOTTED LINES.

**3** NEXT STEP IS EASY. JUST FOLLOW OUR GUIDE LINES FOR HIS BODY

**4** ALMOST DONE! NOW WHEN YOU HAVE THE SHAPE OF THE BAT USE THICKER LINES TO DRAW HIS FINAL SHAPE.

# SHEARS

## DIFFICULTY LEVEL

**1** DRAW TWO WAVY LINES CROSSING EACH OTHER LIKE THE DRAWING ABOVE.

**2** USE THE LINE GUIDES TO DRAW THE SHAPE OF THE SHEARS.

**3** DRAW A JOINING SCREW AT THE CENTER OF THE SHEARS AND ERASE LINE GUIDES.

**4** TO FINISH IT, ADD SOME DETAILS ON HANDLES AND BLADES.

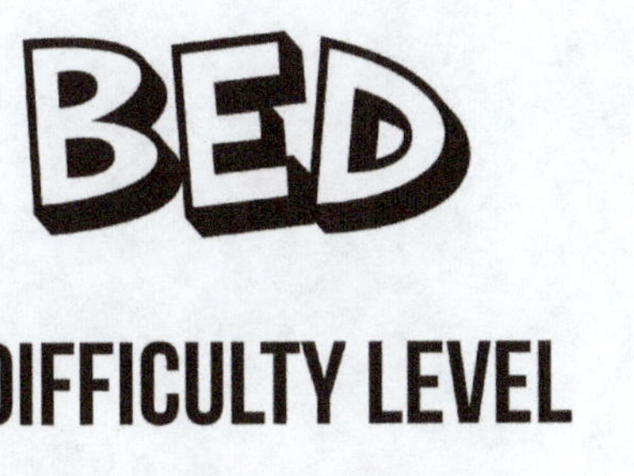


## DIFFICULTY LEVEL

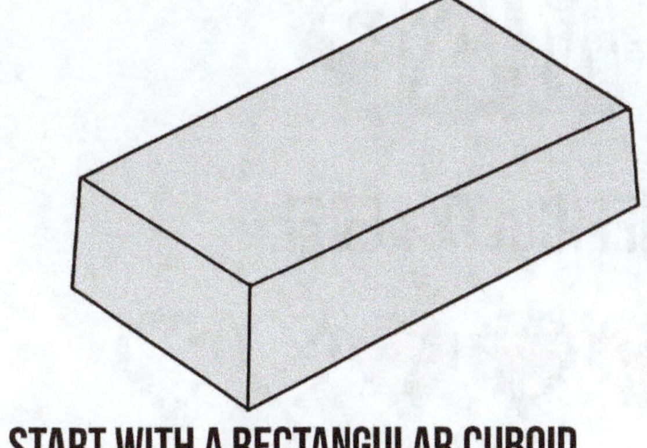

**1** START WITH A RECTANGULAR CUBOID.

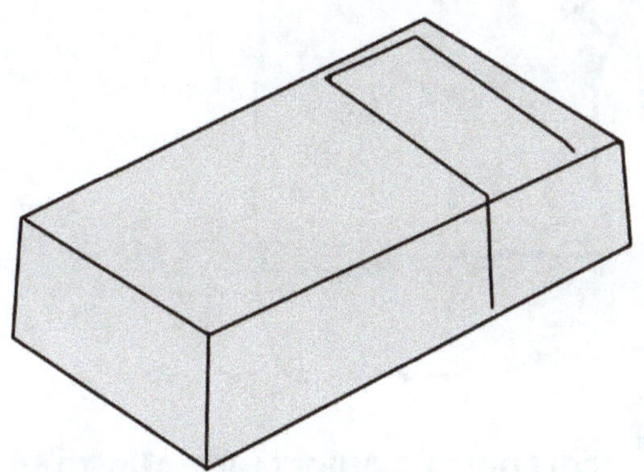

**2** DIVIDE THE CUBOID INTO TWO PARTS.

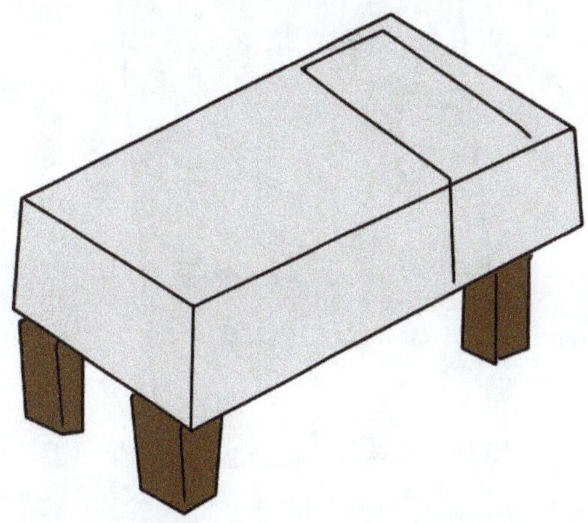

**3** NEXT, DRAW THE FEET OF THE BED.

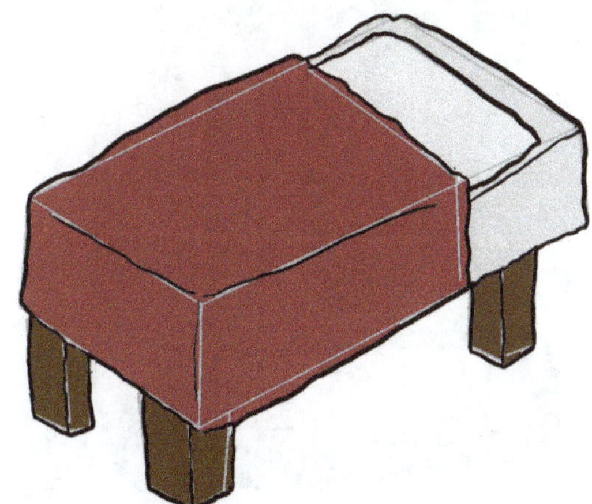

**4** TRACE THE SHAPE OF THE BED AND REMOVE ALL THE LINE GUIDES.

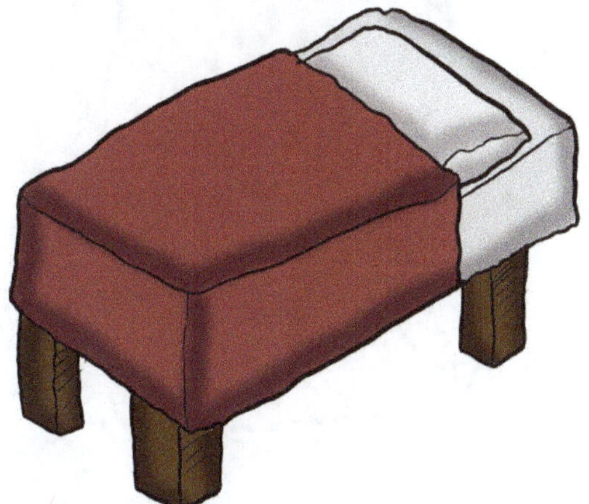

**5** USE THIN LINES AND SHADINGS TO FINISH YOUR DRAWING.

# DIFFICULTY LEVEL

**1** START WITH A RECTANGLE.

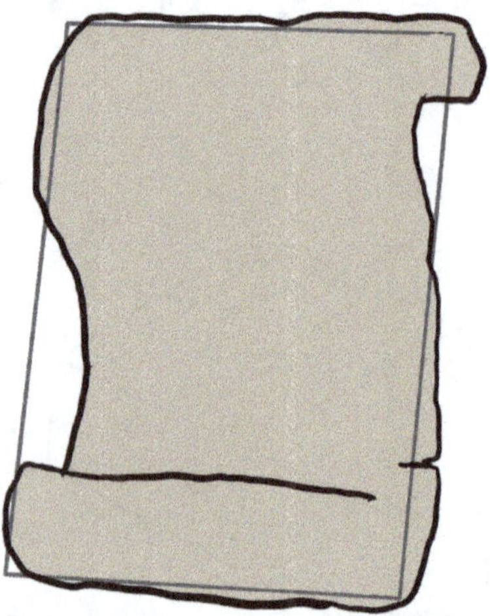

**2** FOLLOW THE GUIDELINES AND TRACE A SHAPE OF THE MAP.

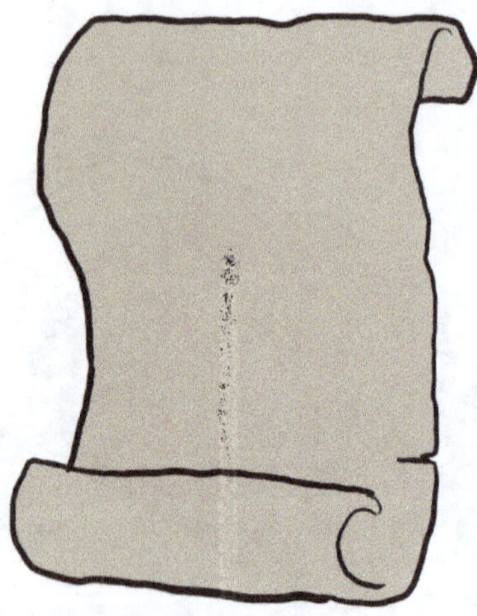

**3** ERASE GUIDELINES AND DRAW WITH THICKER LINES THE FINAL SHAPE OF THE MAP

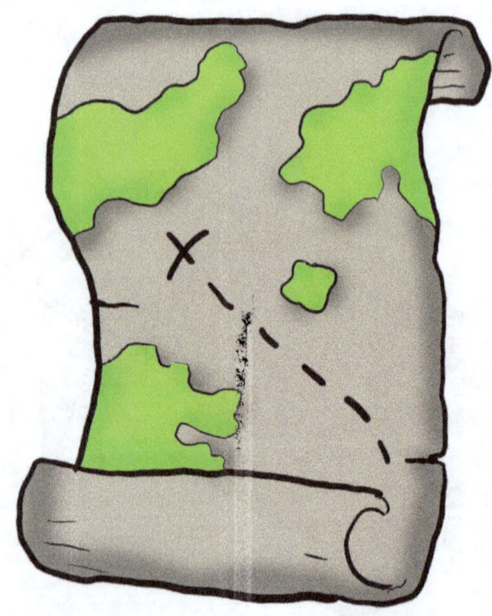

**4** NOW, FINISH YOUR OWN MAP ANY WAY YOU LIKE!

# BOOK

## DIFFICULTY LEVEL

**1** START WITH A RECTANGULAR CUBOID SHAPE.

**2** FOLLOW THE SHAPE AND TRACE A SHAPE OF A BOOK.

**3** ERASE GUIDELINES.

**4** TO FINISH IT, DRAW SOME DETAILS ON THE BOOK COVERS.

DIFFICULTY LEVEL

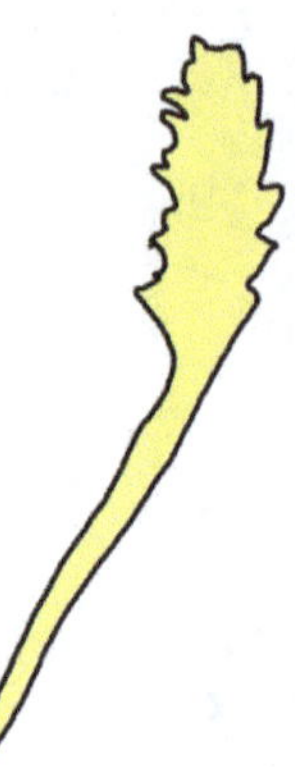

**1** START WITH THIS FUNNY SHAPE.

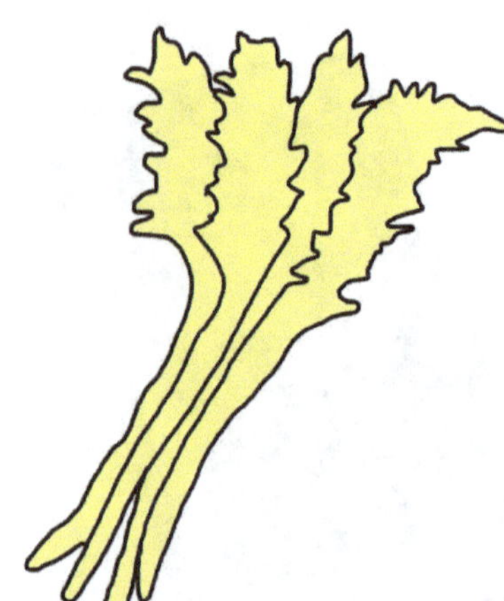

**2** NOW, TRY TO COPY FIRST SHAPE AND DRAW SEVERAL OF THEM FORMING A BUSHEL.

**3** DRAW SOME MORE LEAVES ON TOP AND A CORD AROUND TWIGS.

**4** TRACE OUR GUIDELINES AND DRAW A FINAL SHAPE OF WHEAT BUSHEL.

**5** TO FINISH IT, USE THINNER LINES FOR SOME SMALL DETAILS AND SHADINGS.

# MINECART

## DIFFICULTY LEVEL

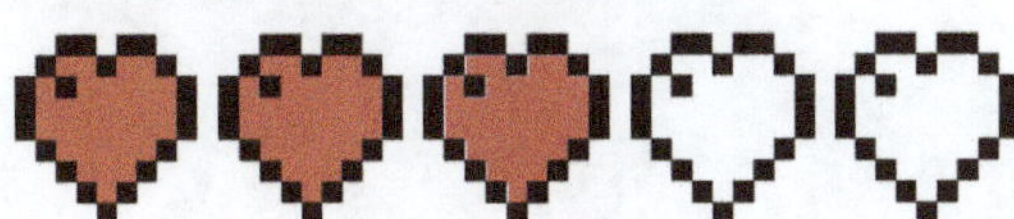

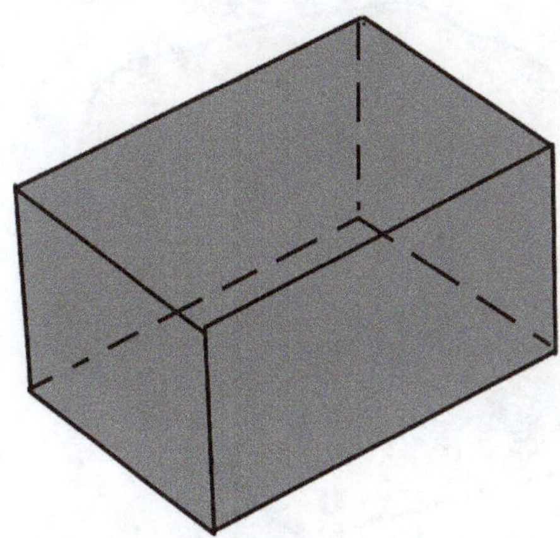

**1** START WITH A RECTANGULAR CUBOID SHAPE .

**2** FORM THE SHAPE OF THE MINECART USING THE GUIDELINES.

**3** ERASE GUIDELINES AND ADD WHEELS ON MINECART.

**4** TO FINISH IT, ADD SOME DETAILS ON EDGES AND SHADINGS.

# PUMPKIN

## DIFFICULTY LEVEL

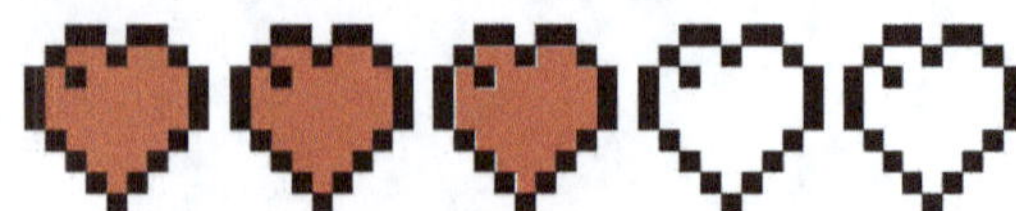

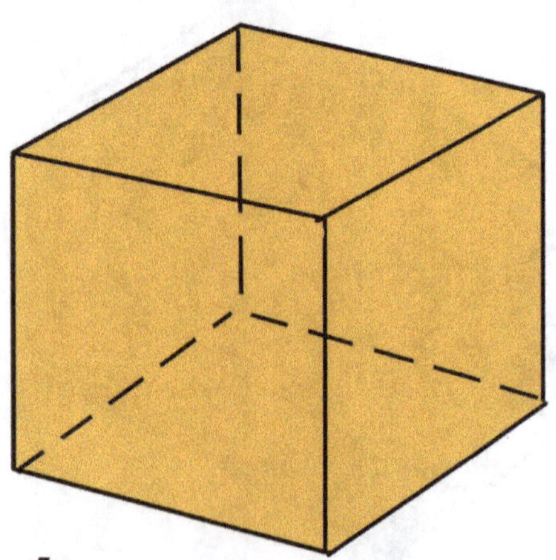

**1** FIRST DRAW A CUBE.

**2** TRACE THE GUIDELINES AND DRAW A PUMPKIN SHAPE. ADD ITS EYES AND MOUTH,

**3** ALMOST DONE, NOW YOU HAVE THE SHAPE OF THE PUMPKIN.

**4** TO FINISH PUMPKIN, DRAW IT A PEDICEL AND SOME SHADINGS.

# DIFFICULTY LEVEL

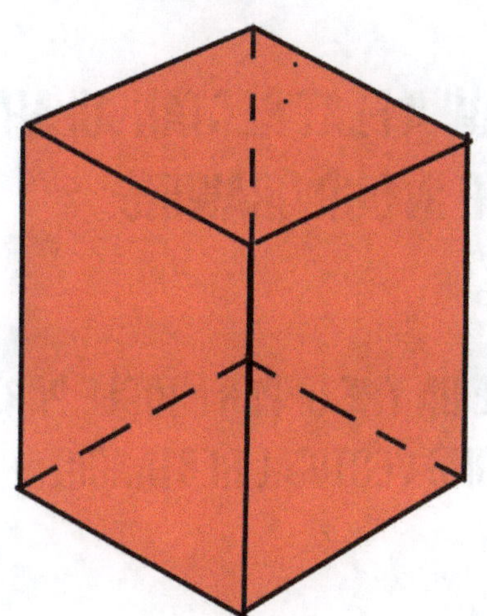

**1** START WITH A LARGE CUBE.

**2** FOLLOW THE DRAWINGS ABOVE AND TRACE THE SHAPE OF THE TNT.

**3** ERASE EXCESSIVE LINES AND DRAW THE LABEL FOR THE TNT.

**4** WRITE TNT ON THE LABEL AND DRAW A FEW WICKS AND IT'S DONE.

# SIGN

## DIFFICULTY LEVEL

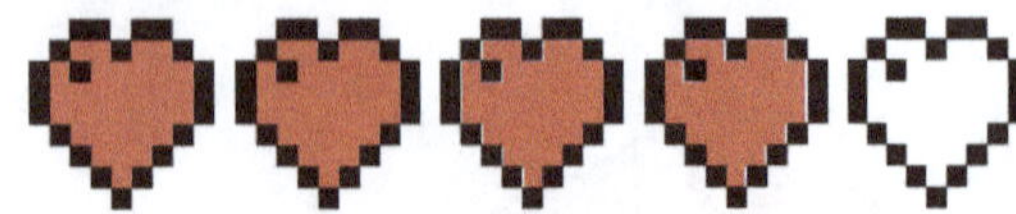

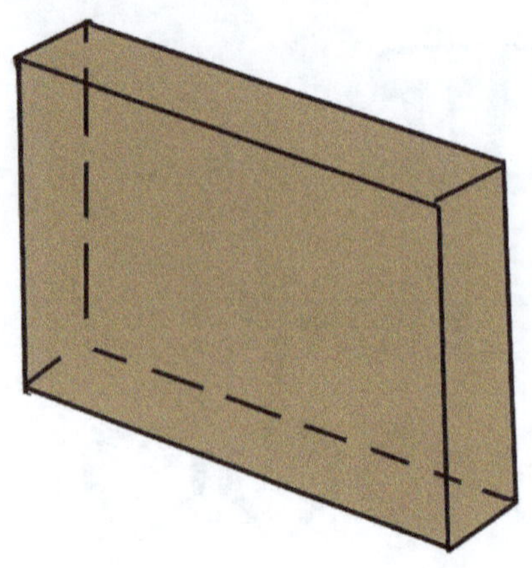

**1** DRAW A FLAT RECTANGULAR CUBOID JUST LIKE IN OUR DRAWING.

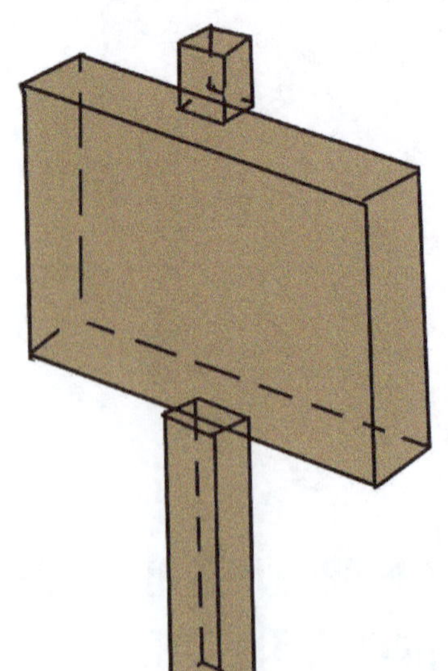

**2** DRAW A SMALL CUBE ON THE UPPER MIDDLE PART OF THE SIGN AND DRAW A LONG VERTICAL RECTANGULAR CUBOID BELOW THE SIGN.

**3** TRACE LINES TO DRAW THE FINAL SHAPE OF OUR SIGN.

**4** DRAW SMALL DETAILS AND SHADING, AND WE HAVE SIGN!

# MUSHROOM

DIFFICULTY LEVEL

**1** FOLLOW THE DRAWING AND START WITH THIS FUNNY LOOKING SHAPE.

**2** DIVIDE THE SHAPE YOU MADE INTO THREE PARTS JUST LIKE THE DRAWING ABOVE.

**3** ADD SPOTS ON IT TO MAKE IT LOOK MORE LIKE A MUSHROOM.

**4** ALMOST DONE NOW! TO FINISH IT, DRAW SOME SMALL DETAILS.

# CHICKEN

## DIFFICULTY LEVEL

**1** FIRST DRAW THE SHAPE OF THE CHICKEN'S HEAD AND TORSO.

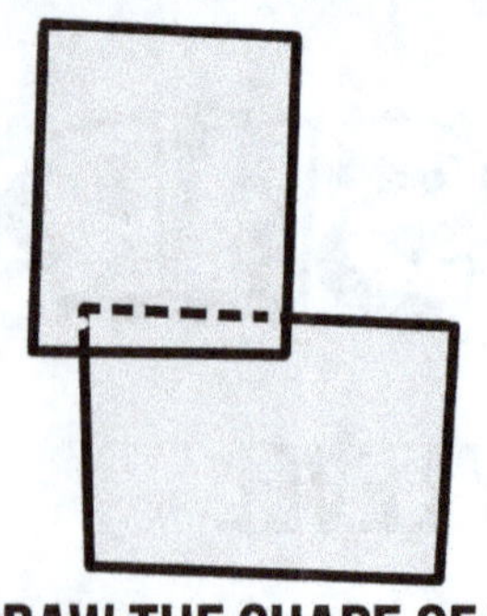

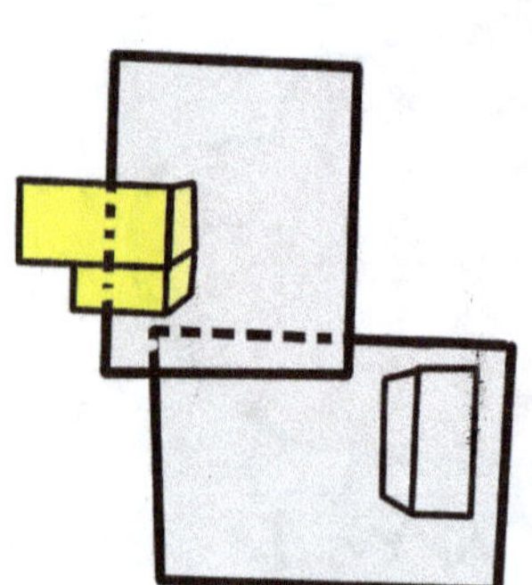

**2** NOW DRAW ITS BEAK AND WING ERASE DOTTED LINES.

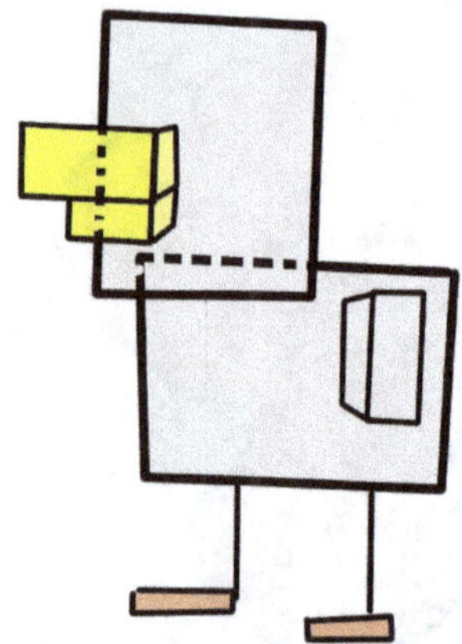

**3** NEXT STEP IS EASY. JUST FOLLOW OUR LEAD AND DRAW ITS LEGS.

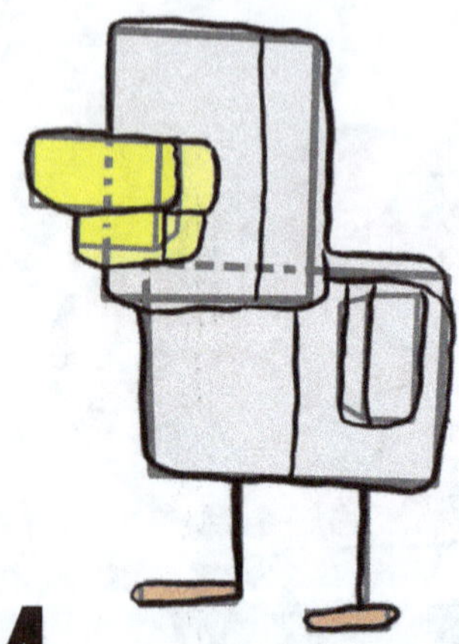

**4** ALMOST DONE! NOW WHEN YOU HAVE THE SHAPE OF THE CHICKEN USE THICKER LINES TO DRAW HIS FINAL SHAPE.

**5** FEW MORE DETAILS AND OUR CHICKEN IS DONE! ADD ITS FACE, SOME SHADING AND IT IS DONE.

# SPRUCE
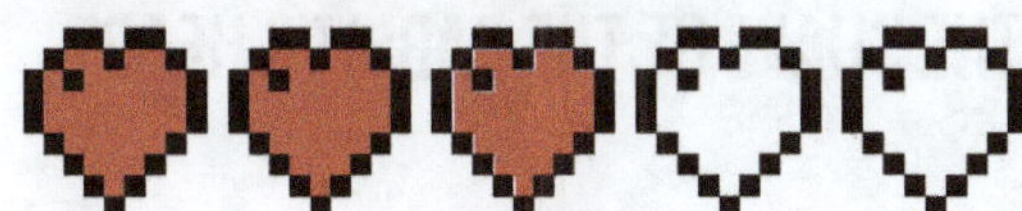

## DIFFICULTY LEVEL

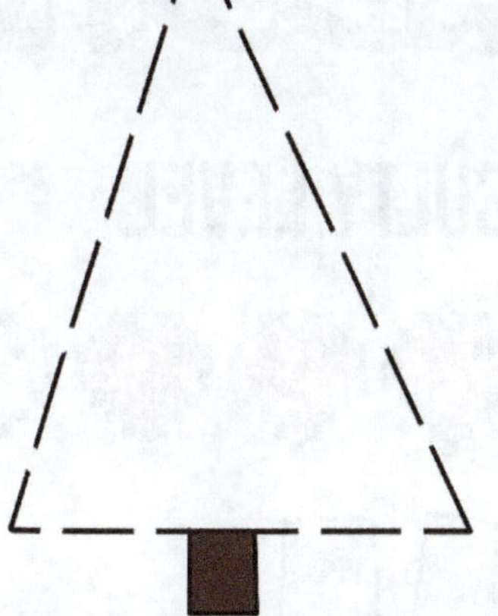

**1** FIRST, DRAW A TRIANGLE WITH A SMALL SQUARE BELOW IT.

**2** DRAW WAVY HORIZONTAL LINES ALONG THE SIDES OF THE TRIANGLE AND FORM THE SHAPE OF THE SPRUCE.

**3** ERASE GUIDELINES AND USE THICKER LINES TO FORM THE SHAPE OF THE SPRUCE.

**4** ADD SOME SMALL DETAILS, AND HERE IT IS!

# RABBIT

## DIFFICULTY LEVEL

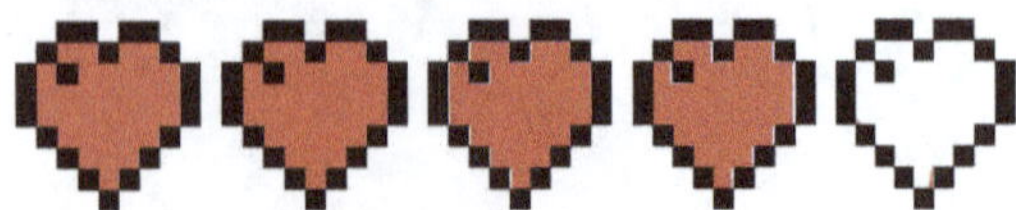

**1** DRAW THE SHAPE OF THE RABBIT'S HEAD AND EARS.

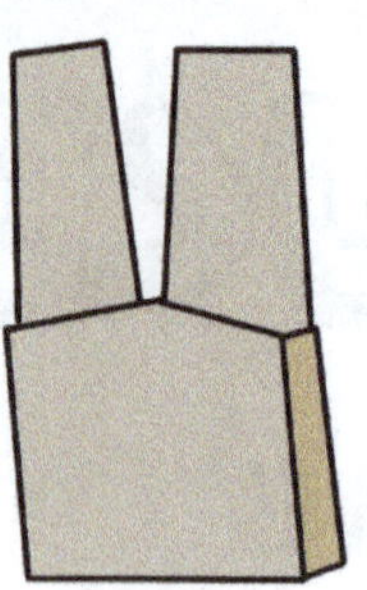

**2** DRAW HIS TORSO AND HIS FRONT LEGS.

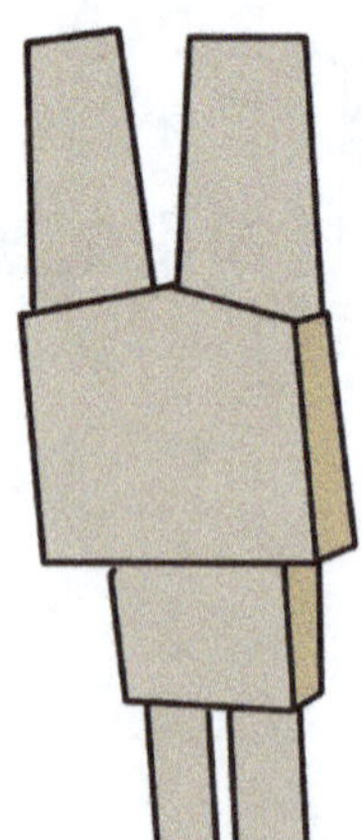

**3** NEXT STEP IS EASY, DRAW HIS BACK LEGS

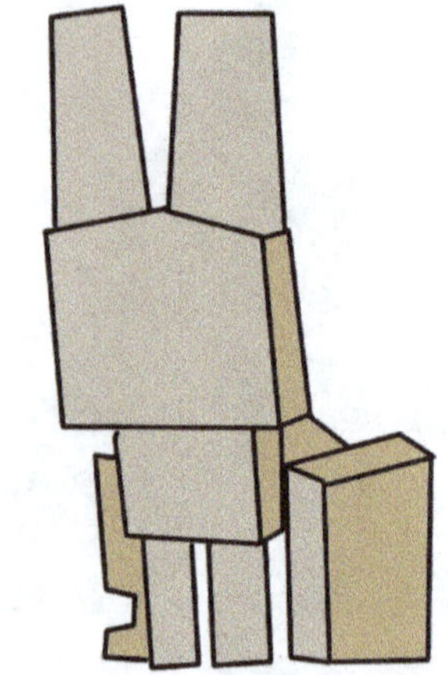

**4** ALMOST DONE! NOW YOU HAVE THE SHAPE OF THE RABBIT.

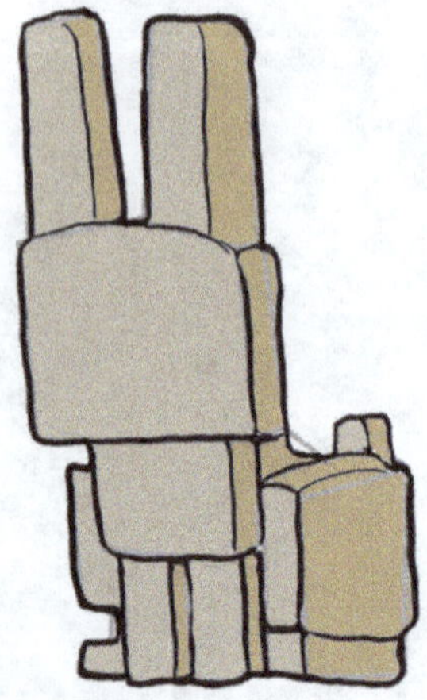

**5** ADD FEW MORE DETAILS AND SHADING, AND OUR RABBIT IS DONE.

# COW

## DIFFICULTY LEVEL

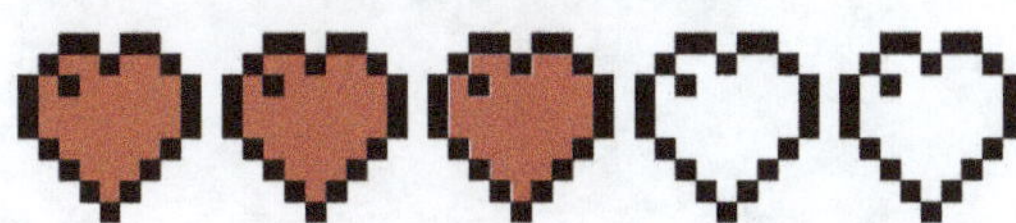

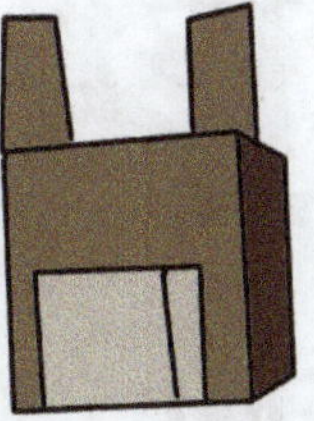

**1** START WITH DRAWING THE COW'S HEAD AND EARS.

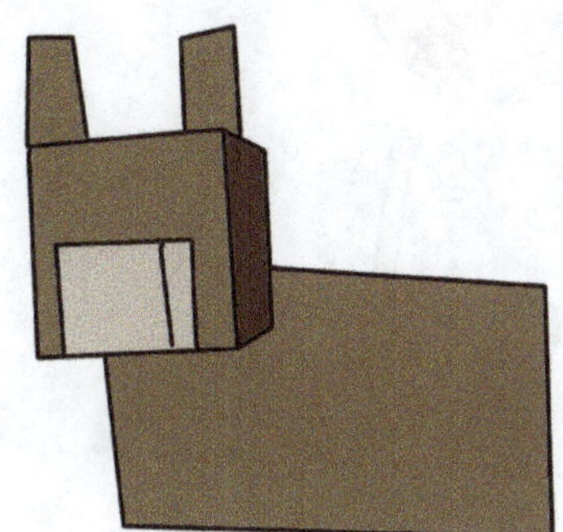

**2** NOW DRAW COW'S TORSO

**3** NEXT STEP IS TO DRAW ITS LEGS

**4** ALMOST DONE! NOW YOU HAVE THE SHAPE OF THE COW.

**5** ADD FEW MORE DETAILS LIKE SPOTS, TAIL AND SOME SHADING. THAT IS IT, COW IS DONE.

# TULIP

## DIFFICULTY LEVEL

**1** FIRST DRAW A STEM.

**2** NEXT DRAW THE SHAPE OF THE FLOWER.

**3** ADD SOME LEAVES.

**4** NOW ADD MORE LEAVES TO OUR PLANT'S STEM.

**5** ADD FEW MORE DETAILS TO BRING OUR TULIP TO LIFE AND ITS DONE.

# SHEEP

## DIFFICULTY LEVEL

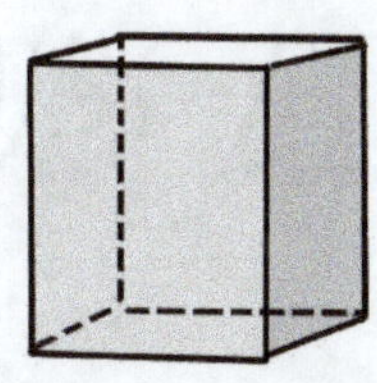

**1** FIRST DRAW THE SHAPE OF THE SHEEP'S HEAD.

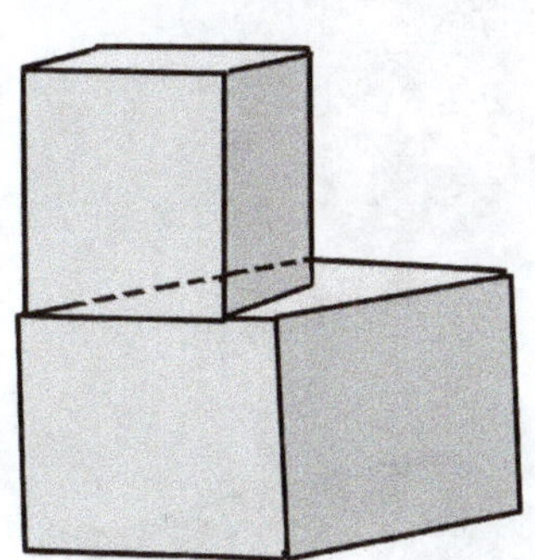

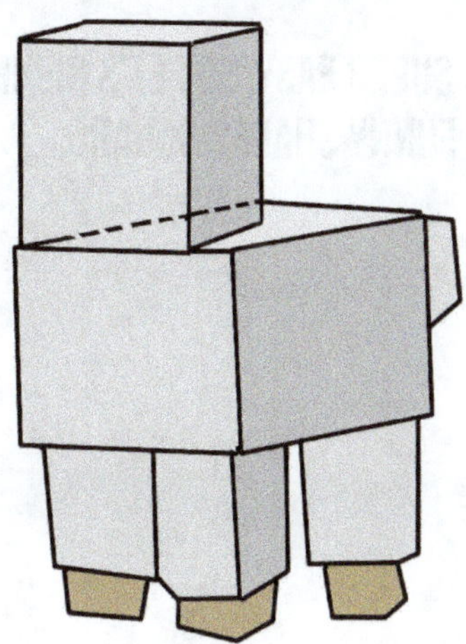

**2** ADD LEGS AND SHEEP'S TAIL

**3** ADD LEGS AND SHEPP'S TAIL

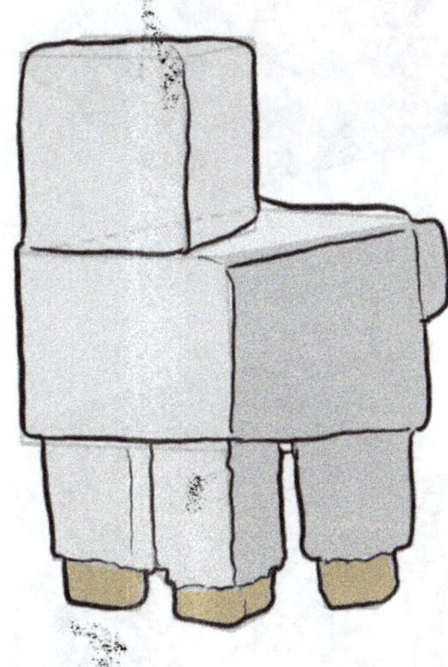

**4** ALMOST DONE, NOW YOU HAVE THE SHAPE OF THE SHEEP.

**5** ADD FACE FEATURES, EARS AND SOME SHADING AND YOU ARE DONE.

# MAGMA CUBE



**1** 1. THIS IS A SUPER EASY, SO LET'S BEGIN. FIRST, DRAW A FUNNY SHAPED SQUARE.

**2** NOW FORM A CUBE BY ADDING THE SIDES OF THE SQUARE.

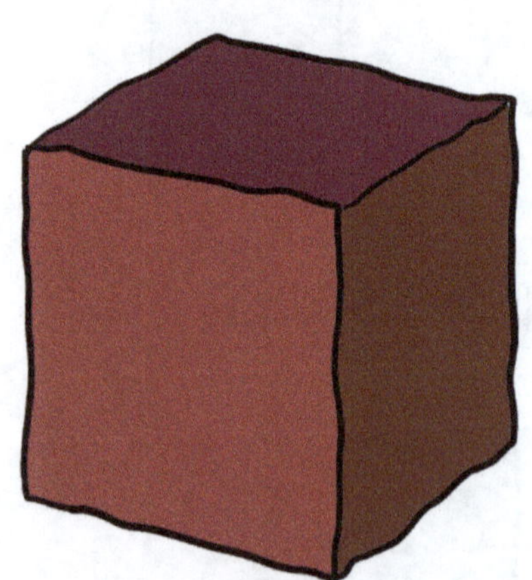

**3** ALMOST DONE! DRAW IT A FACE AND SOME DETAILS TO MAKE YOUR MAGMA CUBE SUPER HOT!

# ALEX

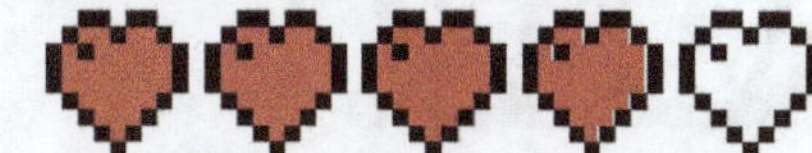

**1** LET'S START OF BY DRAWING ALEX'S HEAD. DRAW A CUBE, THEN ADD THICKER LINES TO THE CUBE AND FINALLY ADD ALEX'S HAIR BANGS AND EAR.

  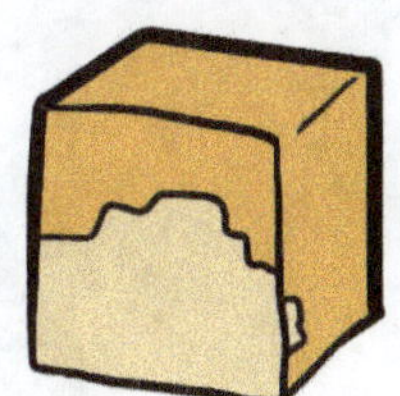

**2** TO MAKE ALEX'S TORSO, DRAW A CUBOID BELOW ALEX'S HEAD. DRAW ALEX'S ARMS AT THE SIDES OF HER TORSO AS YOU CAN SEE IN STEP 2A.

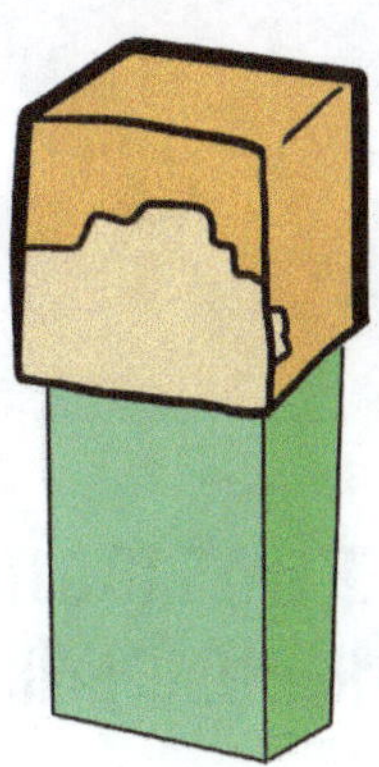

**2 A**

**3** AT THIS STAGE, DRAW TWO RECTANGULAR CUBOIDS BELOW ALEX'S TORSO FOR HER LEGS.

# DIFFICULTY LEVEL

**4** NOW THAT HER BODY IS COMPLETE, LET'S DRAW A SWORD ON HER RIGHT HAND.

**5** USE THICKER LINES TO OUTLINE HER BODY AND ADD HER LONG HAIR TOO

**6** TO FINISH DRAWING ALEX, ADD HER EYES, NOSE AND MOUTH. ADD SOME SHADING AND OTHER DETAILS ON HER CLOTHES AND HAIR.

# DRAGON

**DIFFICULTY LEVEL**

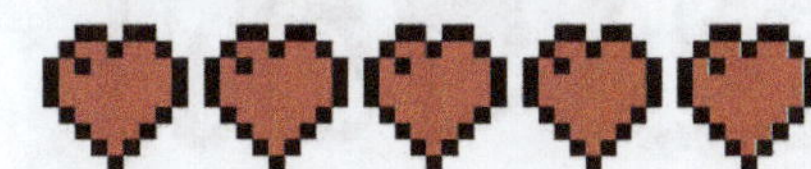

**1** SLET'S START OF BY DRAWING THE DRAGON'S HEAD. BEGIN WITH A BOX SHAPE FOR ITS HEAD AND DRAW ANOTHER BOX FOR ITS SNOUT. THEN DRAW ITS EARS AND NOSTRILS.

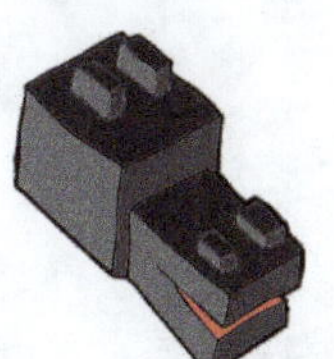

**2** NOW WE CAN DRAW THE DRAGON'S TORSO. START BY DRAWING THE DRAGON'S LONG THIN NECK AND THEN DRAW A LARGE CUBOID FOR ITS BODY. THEN DRAW TWO SMALLER AND THINNER CUBOIDS ON THE SIDES OF THE TORSO TO START OF ITS WINGS.

**3** EXTEND WING BASE BY ADDING THINNER CUBOIDS.

**4** NEXT STEP, DRAW THE DRAGON'S TAIL.

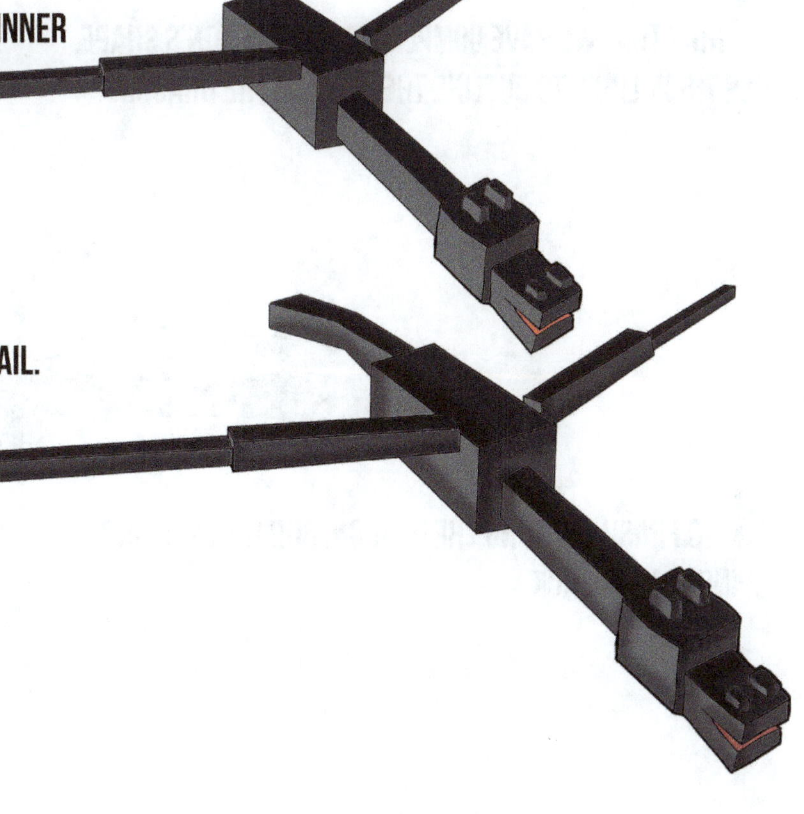

# DRAGON

**DIFFICULTY LEVEL**

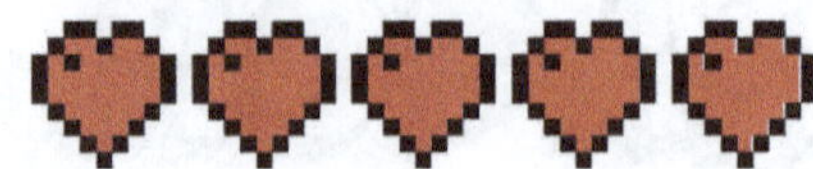

**5** DRAW CURVE AND STRAIGHT LINES ON THE DRAGON'S WINGS TO MAKE IT APPEAR LIKE IT IS FLYING.

**6** DRAW THE LEG OF THE DRAGON AS SHOWN IN THIS STEP.

**7** NOW THAT WE HAVE COMPLETED THE DRAGON'S SHAPE, USE THICK LINES TO OUTLINE THE BODY OF THE DRAGON.

**8** TO FINISH DRAWING THE DRAGON, ADD HIS EYES AND SPINES ON ITS BACK.

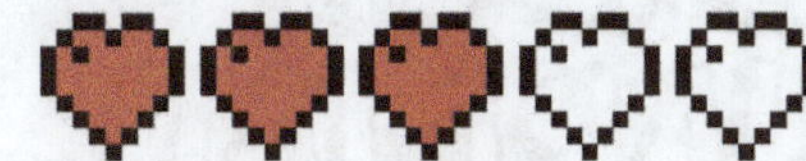

# BAT



**1** START BY DRAWING TWO IRREGULAR SQUARES, WITH THE SMALLER SQUARE ON THE UPPER LEFT PART.
NEXT STEP FOLLOW THE FULL LINE AS SHOWN IN THE IMAGE AND ERASE THE DOTTED LINE. ADD ITS EARS AND TRACE THE OUTLINE OF THE HEAD WITH THICKER LINES.

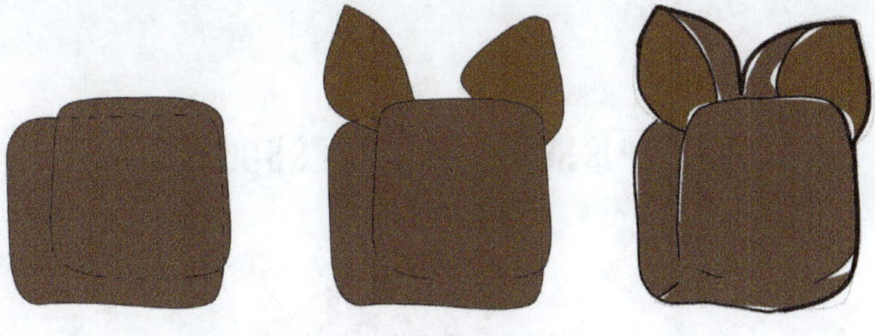

**2** THE NEXT STEP IS TO DRAW A RECTANGULAR PRISM FOR ITS BODY. MAKE SURE THAT THERE'S A LITTLE SPACE IN BETWEEN THE HEAD AND THE BODY TO MAKE IT APPEAR THAT THE HEAD IS PIVOTED. ADD HIS WINGS NEXT.

**3** ALMOST DONE! USE THICKER LINES TO OUTLINE ITS BODY. IN STEP 3A, DRAW HIS EYES, NOSE, TEETH, AND FEET WITH CLAWS.

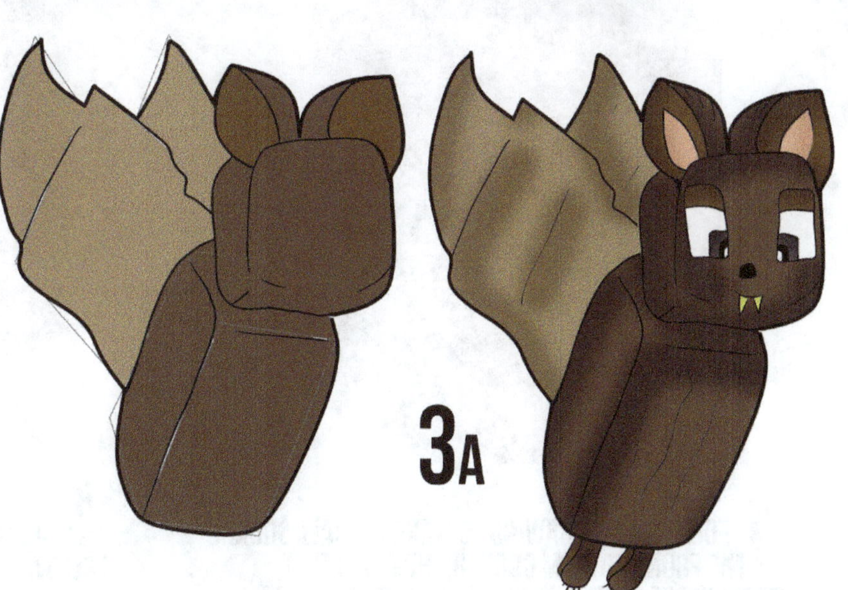

# ENDER GUARDIAN

**1** THIS STEP IS REALLY EASY! LET'S START WITH A LARGE CUBE.

**2** NOW DRAW TWO SQUARES ON THE CUBE AS SHOWN IN THIS IMAGE

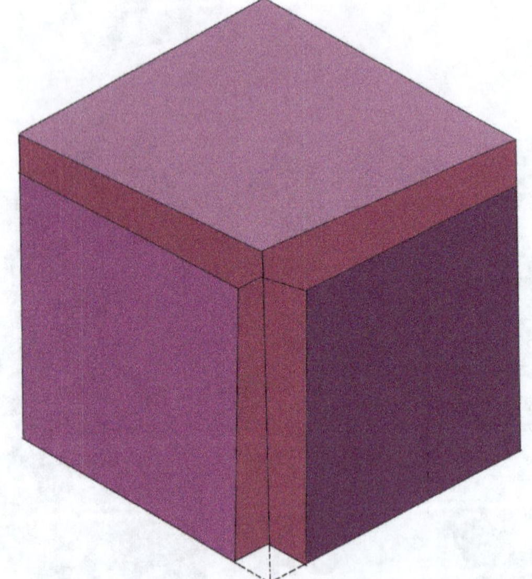

**3** FOLLOW THIS DRAWING TO MAKE A SMALL SQUARE ON THE FRONT BOTTOM CORNER, AND FORM TWO RECTANGLES FACING INSIDE. YOU CAN ERASE DOTTED LINES.

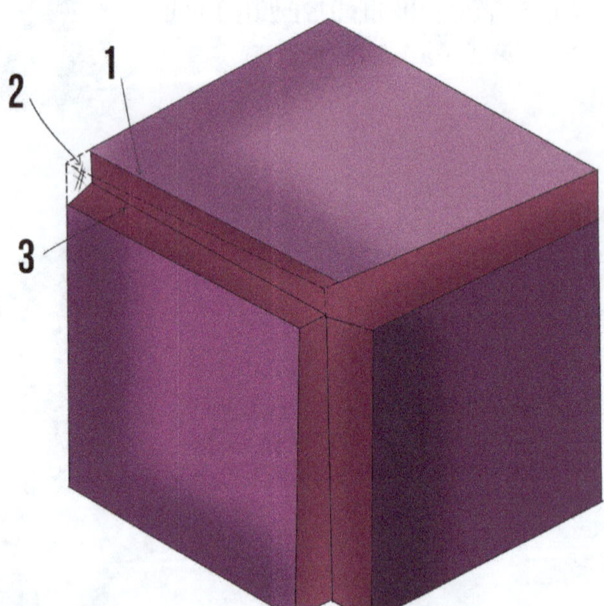

**4** THIS LOOKS COMPLICATED BUT IT IS REALLY EASY JUST FOLLOW THE ILLUSTRATION SHOWN BELOW.

# BREWING STAND

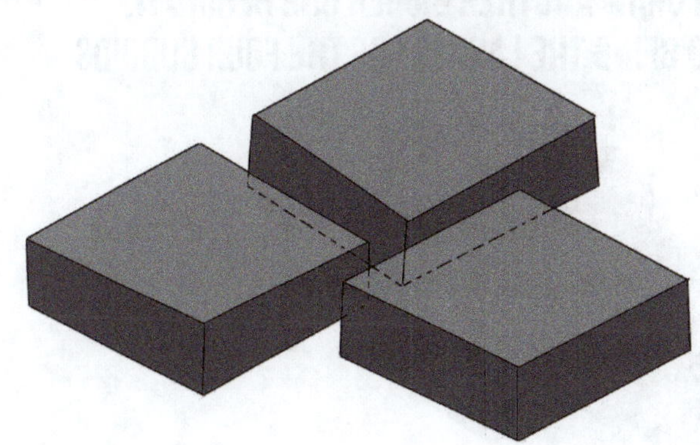

**1** FIRST, DRAW THREE SEPARATE CUBES ADJACENT TO ONE ANOTHER, AND THIS IS GOING TO BE THE BASE OF OUR BREWING STAND. ERASE DOTTED LINES.

**2** DRAW A VERTICAL RECTANGULAR PRISM AT THE MIDDLE OF THE BASE OF THE BREWING STAND.

**3** THIS IS WHAT IT SHOULD LOOK LIKE WHEN YOU ERASE ALL DOTTED LINES IN STEP 2.

# ENDERMITE



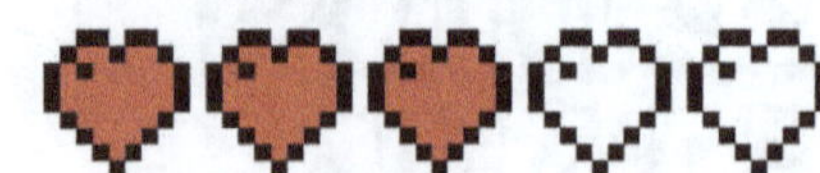

**1** TO DRAW AN ENDERMITE, START WITH A CUBOID, AND DRAW ANOTHER BIGGER ONE BEHIND IT. NEXT DRAW TWO MORE CUBOIDS WITH THE THIRD CUBOID BEING THE LARGEST OF THE FOUR CUBOIDS JUST LIKE IN DRAWING 1A.

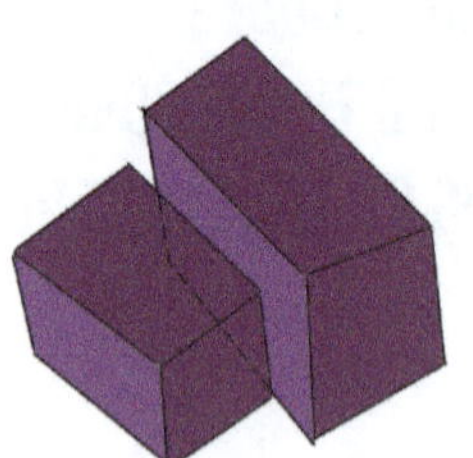

**1A**

**2** CONTINUE STACKING MORE CUBOIDS IN DESCENDING SIZES TO GET THE FINAL SHAPE OF THE ENDERMITES.

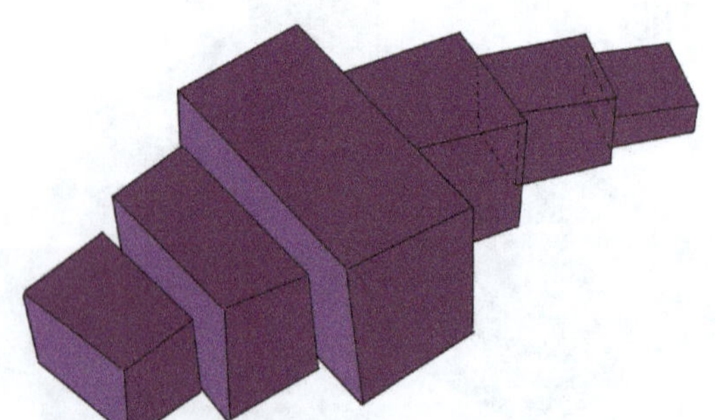

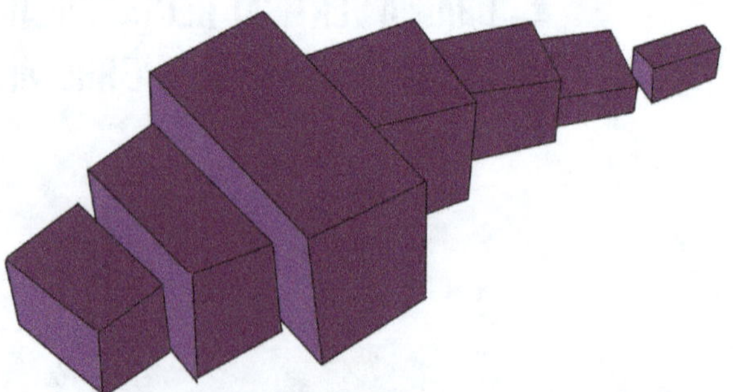

**3** FINALLY, USE THICKER LINES TO OUTLINE THE FINAL SHAPE OF THE ENDERMITES, ADD ITS EYES AND SOME SHADINGS.

# EVOKER

**1** START WITH THIS SHAPE FOR HIS HEAD.

**2** DRAW HIM A NOSE.

**3** DRAW A RECTANGULAR PRISM BELOW HIS HEAD.

# EVOKER

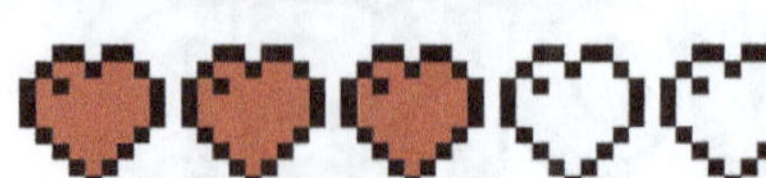

**4** DRAW A HORIZONTAL RECTANGULAR PRISM ACROSS THE UPPER PART OF HIS TORSO.

**5** NEXT, DRAW HIS SHOULDER AS SHOWN IN THIS STEP.

**6** ADD A SMALLER CUBOID BELOW HIS BODY TO MAKE HIS FEET AND REMOVE ALL LINE GUIDES.

**7** NOW YOU CAN TRACE WITH THICKER LINES HIS FINAL SHAPE. DRAW HIS FACE AND DETAILS ON HIS CLOTHING.

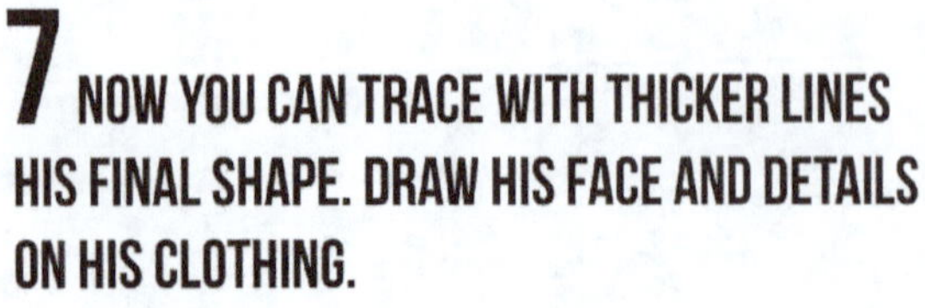
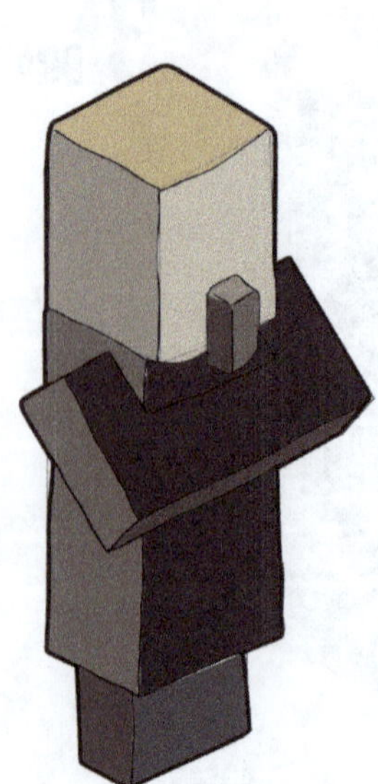

# HORSE

**5** ADD FOUR CUBES BELOW ITS LEGS TO CREATE ITS HOOFS. DRAW ITS TAIL AS WELL.

**6** TRACE THE OUTLINE OF THE HORSE WITH THICKER LINES TO FORM THE FINAL SHAPE OF THE HORSE

**7** NOW FINISH DRAWING YOUR HORSE BY ADDING ITS EYES AND DRAWING ITS THICK MANE.

# INFINITE FIRE



**1** START WITH THIS SHAPE:

**2** NOW, DRAW A FLAME AND A SIDE OF THE BOWL WHICH HOLDS AN INFINITE FIRE.

**3** DRAW THE FLAME AND THE SIDE OF THE BOWL WHICH HOLDS THE FIRE.

# CHICKEN

**1** LET'S DRAW THIS CHICKEN. START WITH THE BODY — A LARGE CUBE. THEN LIKE IN IMAGE 1A DRAW A RECTANGLE ABOVE THE CUBE. THEN ADD A DIMENSION TO THE RECTANGLE TO MAKE IT LOOK LIKE A PRISM.

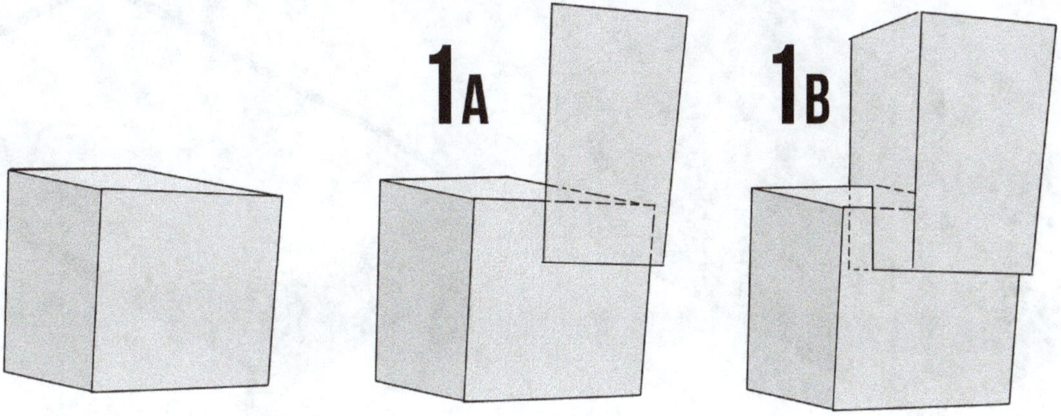

**2** DRAW THE CHICKEN'S WING, FOLLOWED BY ITS BEAK AND FINALLY ITS WADDLE.

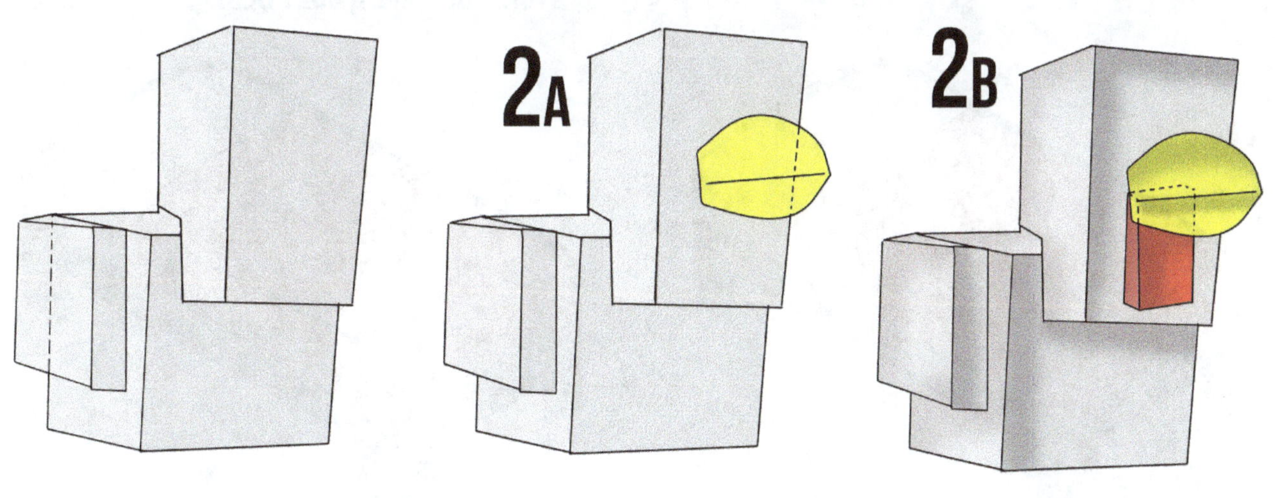

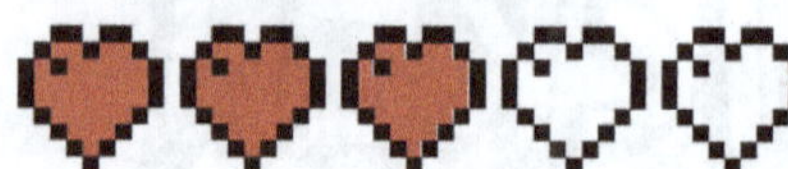

**1** LET'S START WITH THIS SHAPE. IT IS A LARGE RECTANGULAR PRISM.

**2** SHAPE YOR BED AND ITS LEGS BY FOLLOWING NEXT SIMPLE STEP. ERASE DOTTED LINE.

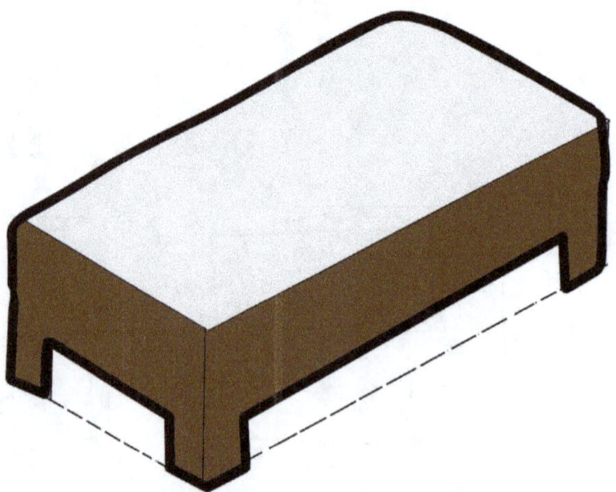

**3** ALMOST DONE! NOW YOU CAN DRAW THE BLANKET AND SEPARATE THE PARTS OF THE BED.

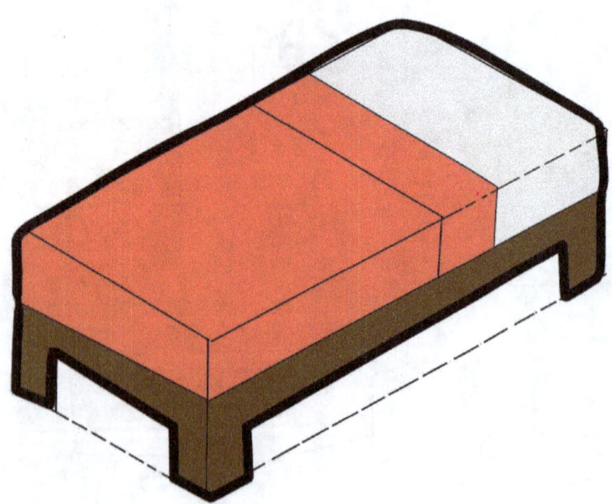

**4** ALMOST DONE! USE THINNER LINES TO DRAW PILLOW AND SMALL DETAILS, AND YOU HAVE A COZY BED!

# ENDERMAN

**1** START BY DRAWING A CUBE FOR THE ENDERMAN'S HEAD.

**2** DRAW A RECTANGULAR PRISM BELOW THE ENDERMAN'S HEAD TO CREATE ITS TORSO.

**3** DRAW HIS LONG ARMS AS SHOWN IN THE IMAGE.

# ENDERMAN

**4** NOW — DRAW THE ENDERMAN'S LONG SLENDER LEGS AND A BLOCK IN BETWEEN HIS ARMS.

**5** ALMOST DONE! TRACE WITH THICKER LINES THE OUTLINE OF THE ENDERMAN'S BODY AND THE BLOCK HE IS HOLDING.

**6** TO FINISH YOUR ENDERMAN, DRAW HIM A FACE. SHADINGS AND ADDITIONAL DETAILS WILL MAKE HIM REALLY COOL.

# GHAST


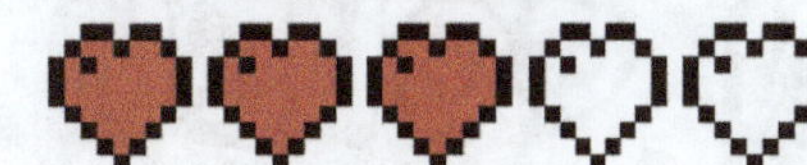

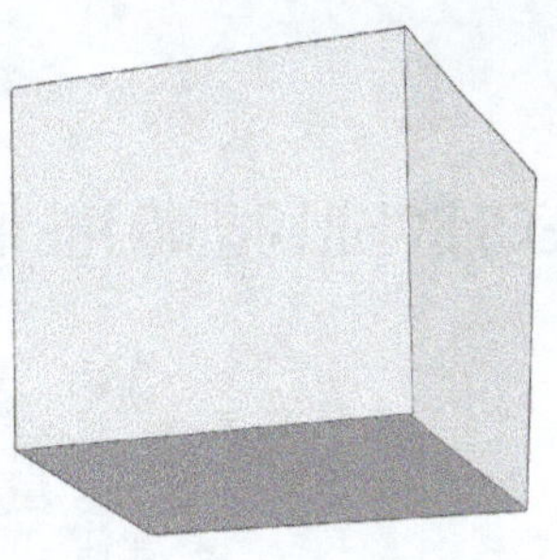
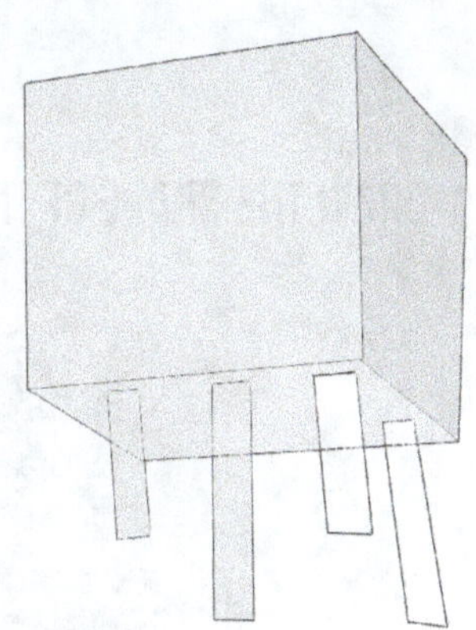

**1** TO DRAW A GHAST, FOLLOW THESE STEPS. FIRST, DRAW A CUBE, AFTER THAT DRAW SMALL RECTANGLES FOR ITS LEGS.

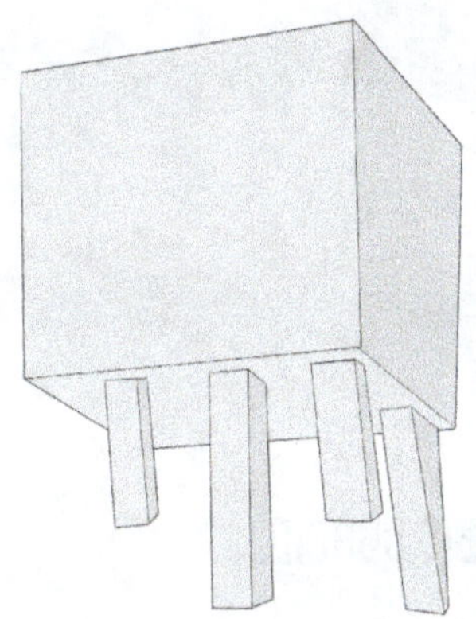
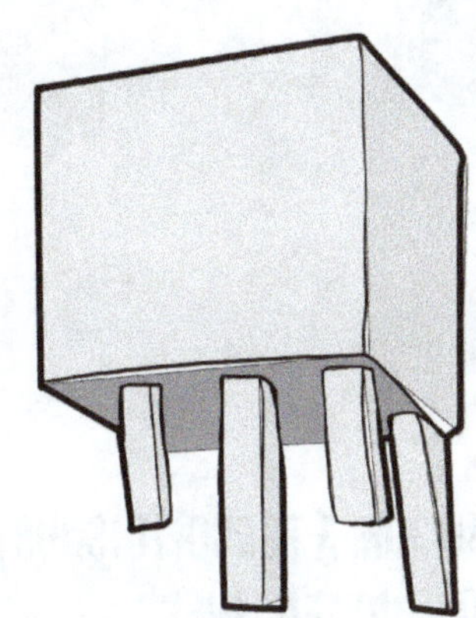

**2** MAKE HIS LEGS REALISTIC BY DRAWING ITS SIDES JUST LIKE IN THE LEFT PICTURE.

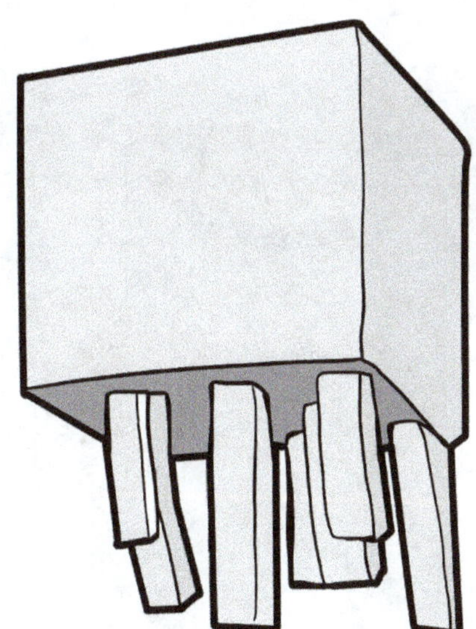

**3** LET'S DRAW THIS GHAST EVEN MORE LEGS AND USE THICKER LINES TO TRACE THE FINAL SHAPE OF THE GHAST AND ITS LEGS.

**4** TO FINISH IT, JUST DRAW IT A FACE AND SOME LINES FOR SHADING. COOL, ISN'T IT?

# IRON GOLEM

**1** DRAW THE SHAPE OF ITS HEAD BY FOLLOWING THE ILLUSTRATIONS BELOW.

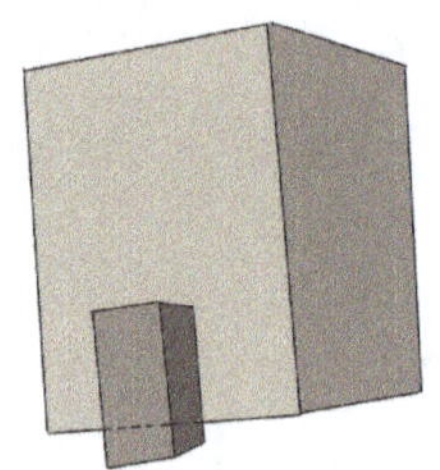

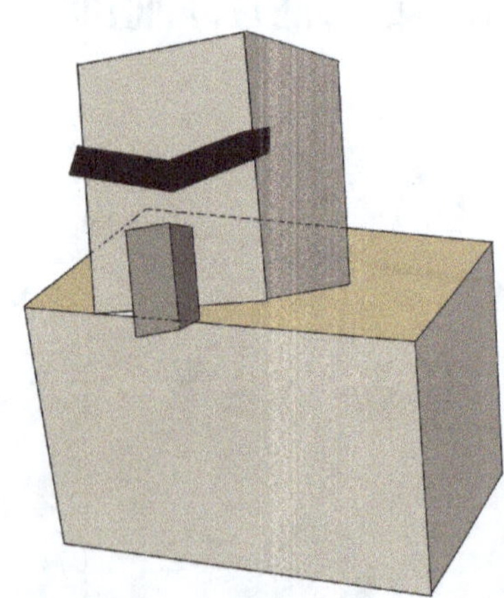

**2** DRAW HIM A TORSO. IT IS JUST A BIG CUBOID. ERASE ALL DOTTED LINES.

**3** NOW HANDS! START WITH ITS SHOULDERS, AND DRAW TWO LONG RECTANGLES ON ITS SIDES.

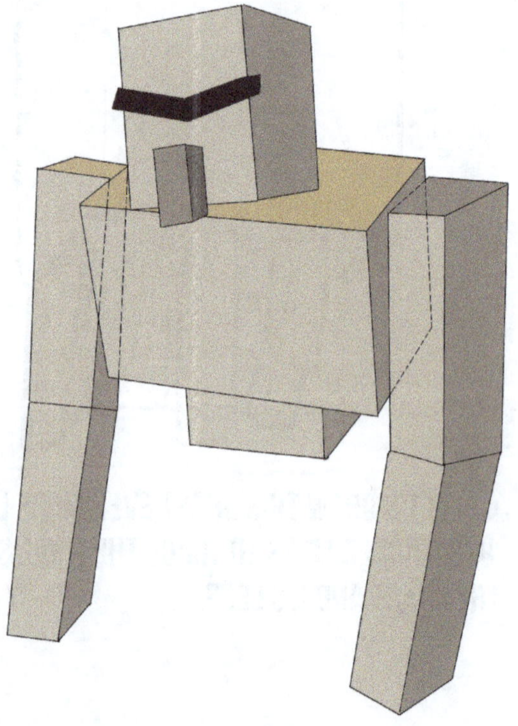

# LLAMA

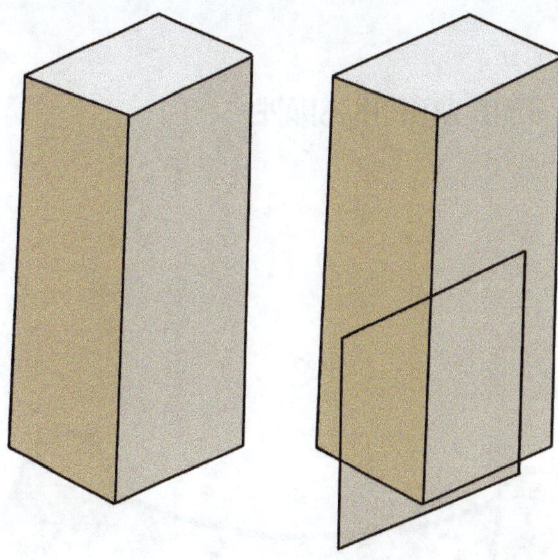

**1** LET'S START WITH A LARGE CUBOID AND THEN DRAW A SMALLER SQUARE IN FRONT OF THE LARGE CUBOID AS SHOWN IN THE DRAWING TO THE RIGHT.

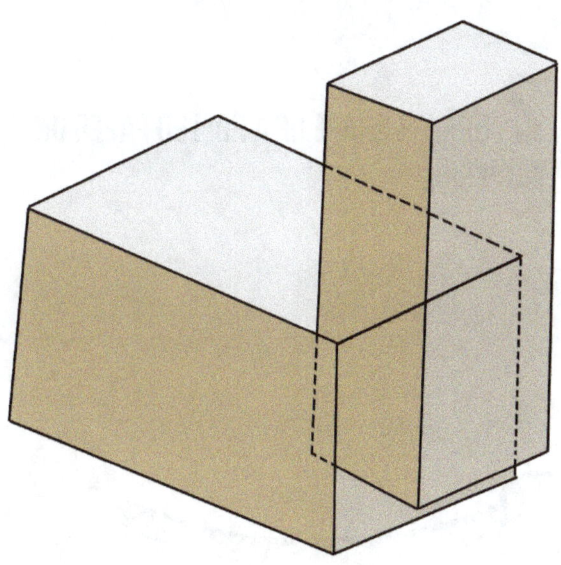

**2** ADD DIMENSIONS TO THE SQUARE TO MAKE IT A RECTANGULAR PRISM. ERASE DOTTED LINES.

**3** WHEN YOU ERASE GUIDELINES, YOU SHOULD HAVE A SHAPE LIKE THIS ONE.

## DIFFICULTY LEVEL

**1** START WITH THIS SHAPE:

**2** DRAW A SHAPE OF A ROLLED PAPER ON EACH SIDE.

**3** ALMOST DONE! NOW YOU CAN FINISH YOUR MAP WITH SOME SMALL DETAILS ON THE SIDES, AND OF COURSE, DRAW ANY KIND OF SECRET TREASURE MAP!

# MOOSHROOM

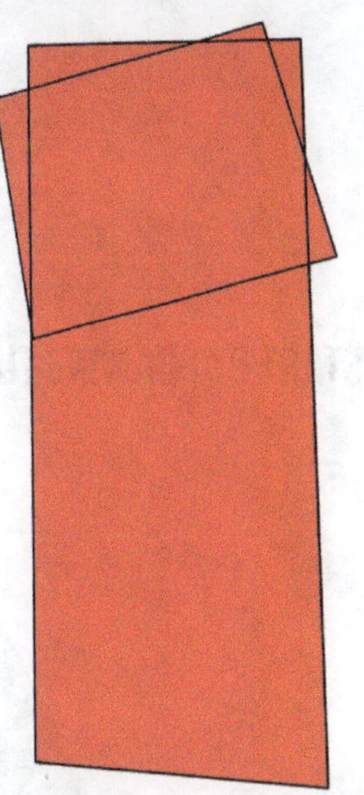

**1** START BY DRAWING A SQUARE DRAWN OVER A VERTICAL RECTANGLE. THE SQUARE IS DRAWN ON AN ANGLE AND IS NOT PARALLEL TO THE RECTANGLE.

**2** NOW, ON THE UPPER CORNER OF THE SQUARE DRAW THE MOOSHROOM'S HORNS AND ADD A HORIZONTAL RECTANGLE ACROSS THE LOWER PART OF THE SQUARE TO CREATE THE MOOSHROOM'S SNOUT.

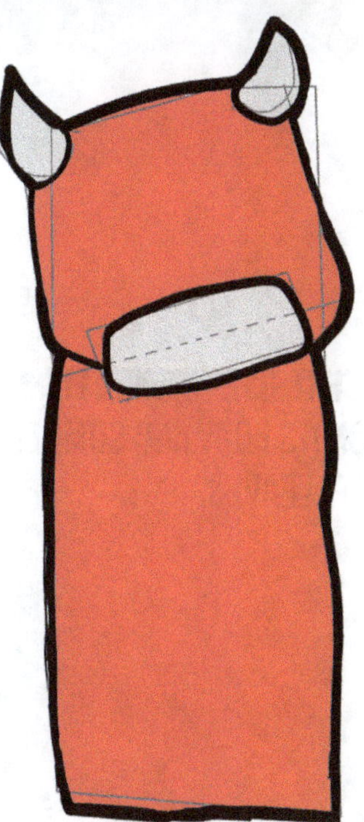

**3** DRAW THE MOOSHROOM'S HEAD AND BODY AND REMOVE GUIDELINES.

**1** START BY DRAWING THE SHAPE OF THE CARROT.

**2** ADD ITS LEAVES.

**3** TO FINISH IT, USE THINNER LINES TO DRAW WRINKLES ON ITS BODY AND SOME LINES TO SEPARATE ITS LEAVES.

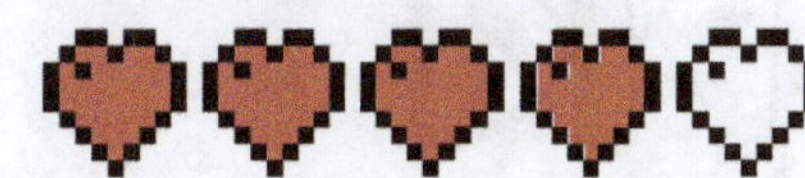

# PARROT

**1** TO DRAW A PARROT'S HEAD, FOLLOW THE ILLUSTRATIONS SHOWN BELOW. ERASE DOTTED LINES FOR THE NEXT STEP.
2.

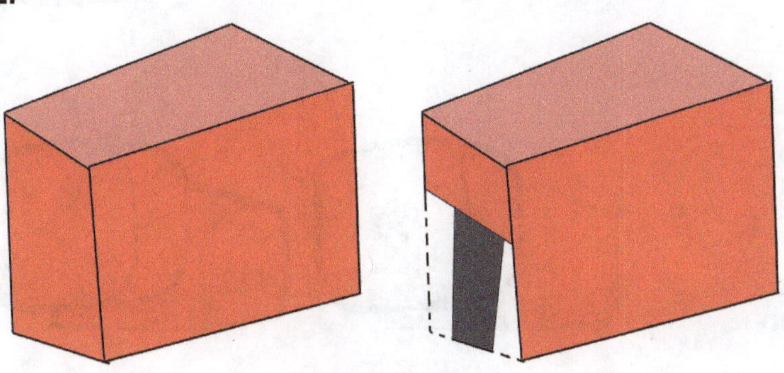

**2** LET'S DRAW ITS BEAK! FIRST, FORM A SMALL TRAPEZOID FOLLOWING STEP 1. THAN DRAW A LINE FROM THE MARKED POINT. AND FOR THE LAST STEP DRAW THE LOWER PART OF THE BEAK.

**3** NOW YOU CAN FINISH THE SHAPE OF ITS HEAD BY ADDING TALONS ON TOP OF IT.

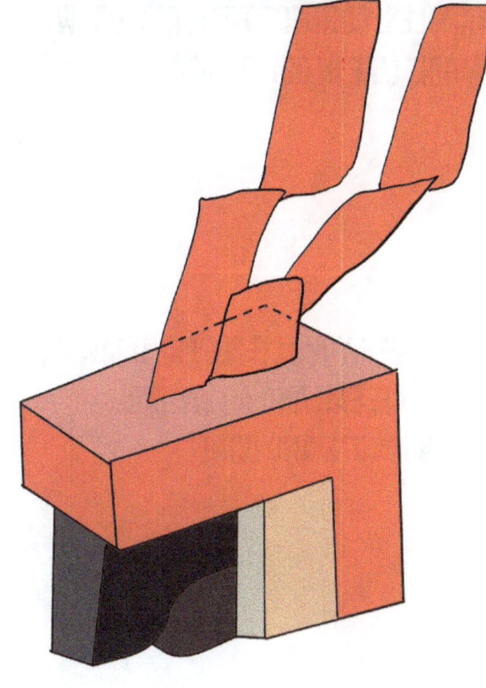

# PIG

**DIFFICULTY LEVEL**

**1** START FROM THIS SHAPE TO DRAW PIG'S HEAD.

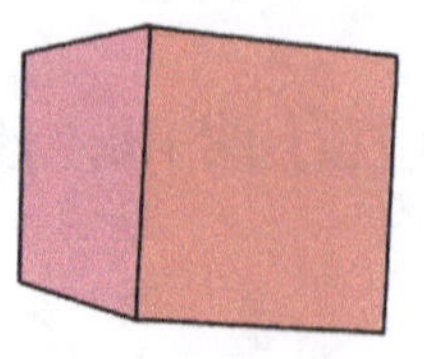

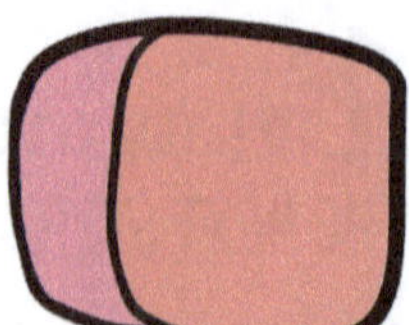

**2** IN THIS STEP, DRAW ITS TORSO

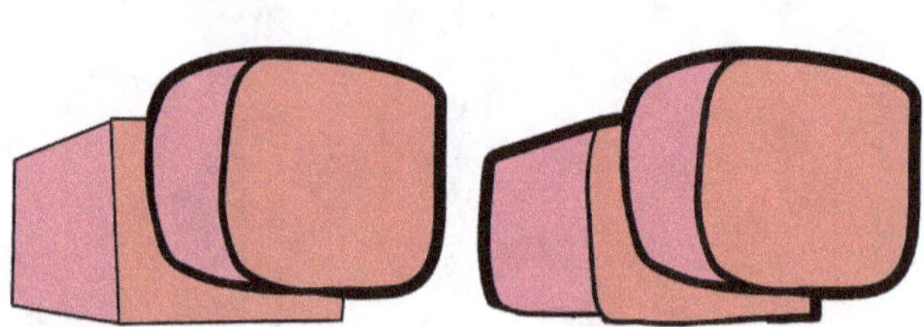

**3** NOW, LEGS.  START WITH 3 SEPARATE RECTANGLES, CONNECT THEM AND DRAW ONE MORE  LIKE IN OUR DRAWING.

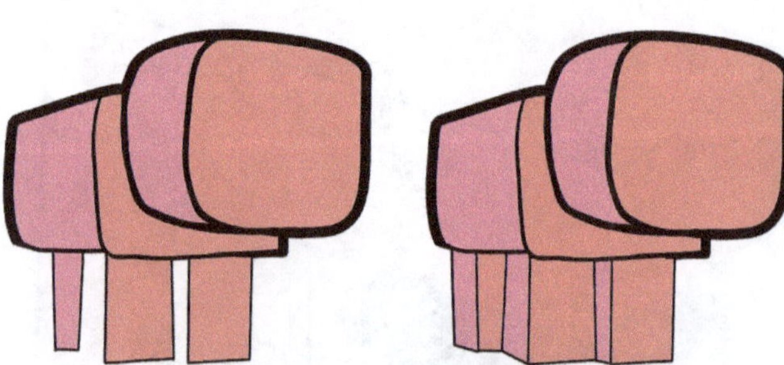

**4** TO FINISH YOUR LITTLE PIG, DRAW IT A CUTE FACE, EAR AND A TINY TAIL. YOUR PIG IS CUTE AND DONE!

# ENDER-CHEST



**1** TO FORM THE SHAPE OF AN ENDER-CHEST, LET'S START WITH ONE BIG, BORING CUBE!

**2** DRAW TWO LINES TO SEPARATE ITS TOP FROM THE BOTTOM.

**3** NOW, LET'S DRAW IT A LOCK. IT LOOKS LIKE A SMALL RECTANGULAR CUBOID, LYING AT THE MIDDLE LINE WHICH SEPARATES THE TOP FROM THE BOTTOM.

**4** ALMOST DONE! NOW YOU CAN FINISH YOUR IMAGE BY ADDING DETAILS ON YOUR ENDER-CHEST.

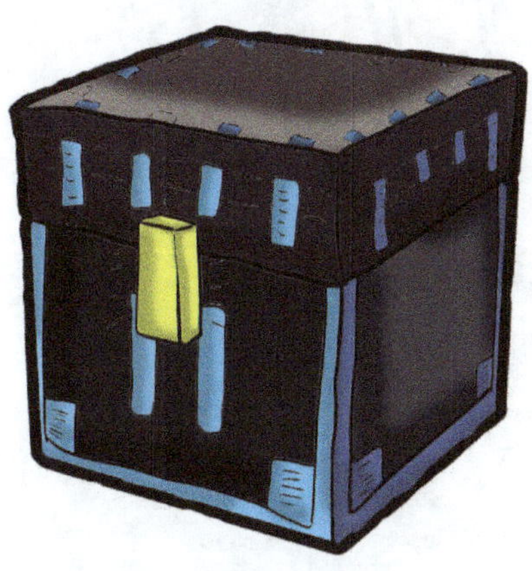

**1** FOLLOW THESE THREE EASY STEPS TO FORM THIS RABBIT'S HEAD.

**2** NEXT DRAW THE RABBIT'S BODY BY OLLOWING THE SHAPE SHOWN IN THIS IMAGE. ERASE DOTTED LINES.

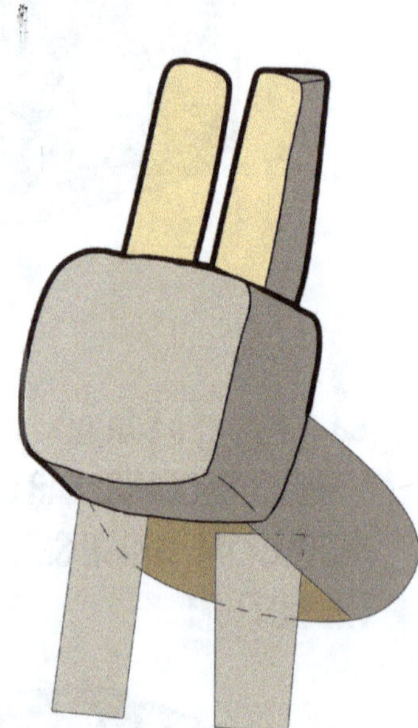

**3** NOW, DRAW THE OUTLINE OF HIS LEGS BY DRAWING TWO RECTANGLES.

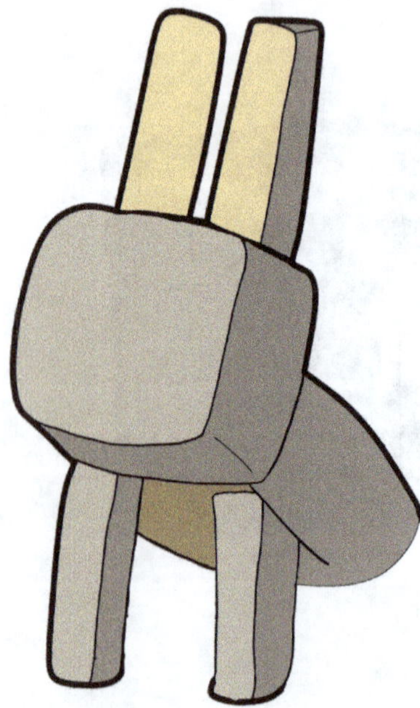

**4** DRAW THE SIDES OF THE LEGS TO ADD DIMENSION TO THE DRAWING.

# POLAR BEAR



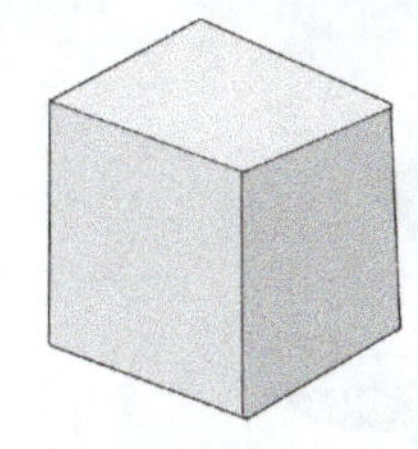
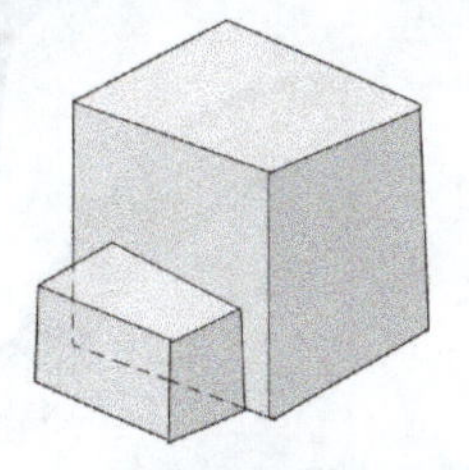
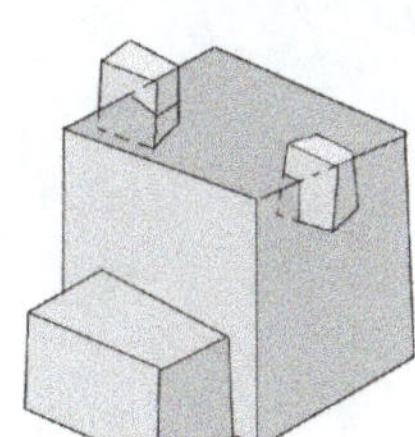
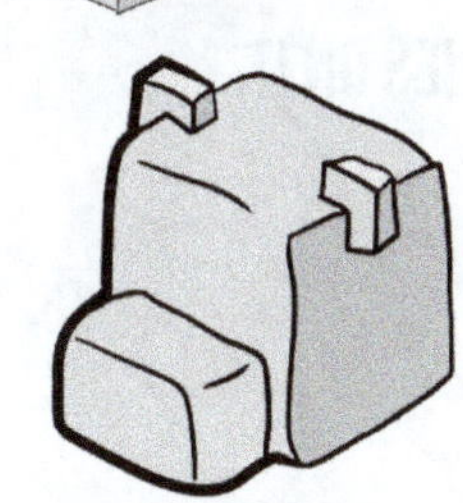

**1** START WITH A CUBE TO FORM THE POLAR BEAR'S HEAD. ADD A SMALL RECTANGULAR PRISM TO FORM ITS MOUTH AND FINALLY DRAW TWO SMALLER CUBES TO FORM ITS EARS. TRACE THE HEAD WITH THICKER LINES.

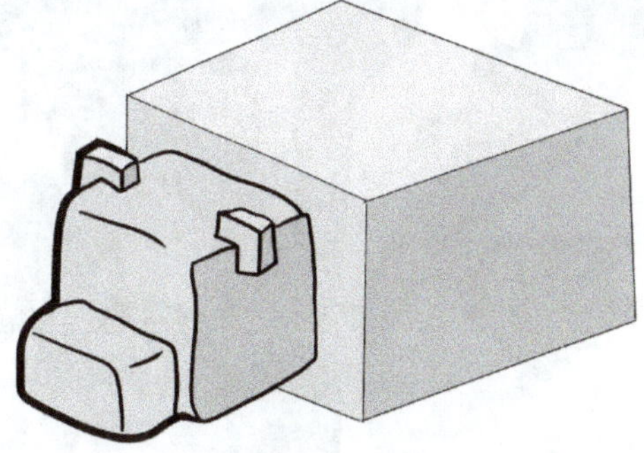

**2** TO DRAW THE TORSO, ADD A BIG CUBOID BEHIND THE BEAR'S HEAD JUST LIKE WHAT IS SHOWN IN THE DRAWING.

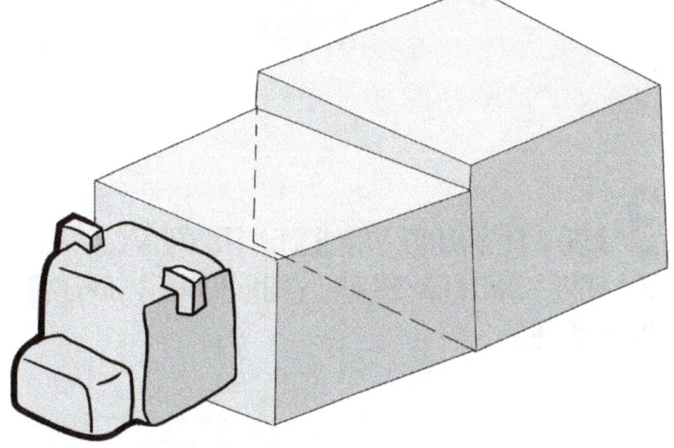

**3** NOW UNTO THE SECOND PART OF THE TORSO, DRAW A BIGGER SHAPED CUBE BEHIND THE FIRST PART OF THE TORSO. USING ONE OF THE EDGES AS BASELINE.

# RUBBER SAPLING

**DIFFICULTY LEVEL**

**1** START WITH THE SHAPE OF THE SAPLING.
FIRST DRAW THE MAIN TRUNK AND DRAW FEW BRANCHES ON IT.

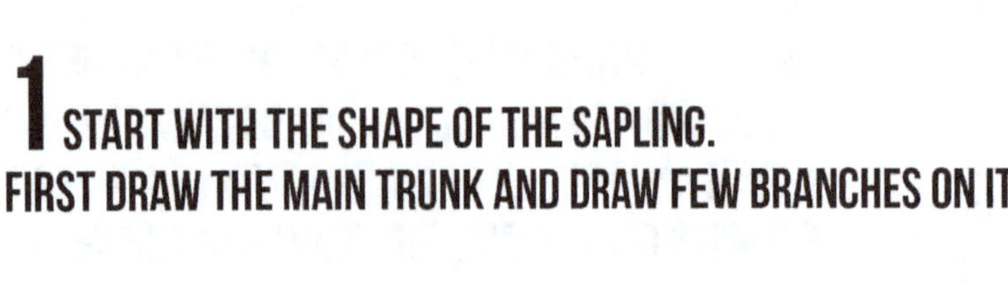

**2** ADD LEAVES ON ITS BRANCHES.

**3** ADD A FEW MORE DETAILS ON ITS TRUNK,
BRANCHES AND LEAVES AND YOUR RUBBER SAPLING
IS FINISHED.

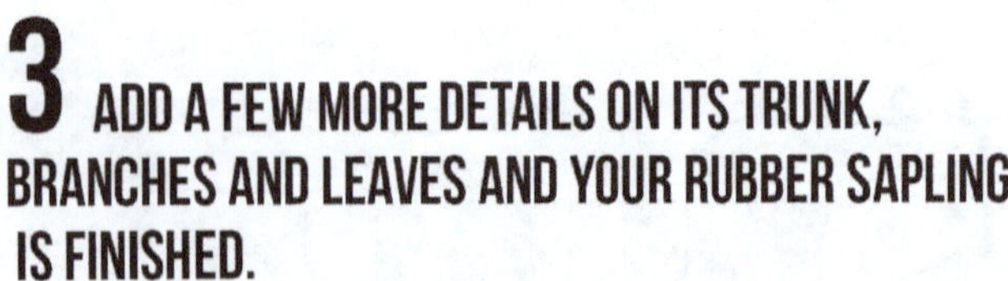

# SHULKER


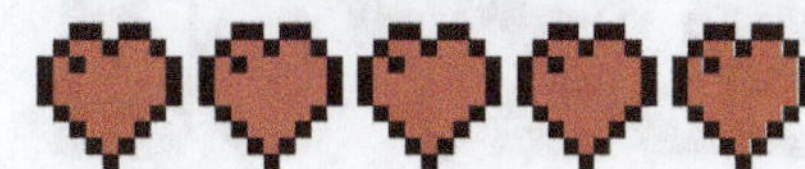

**1** 1. START WITH SHAPING HIS UPPER PART AND FOLLOWING THESE STEPS.

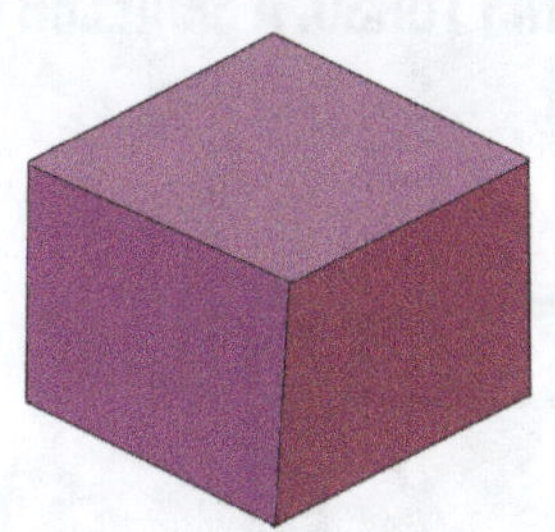 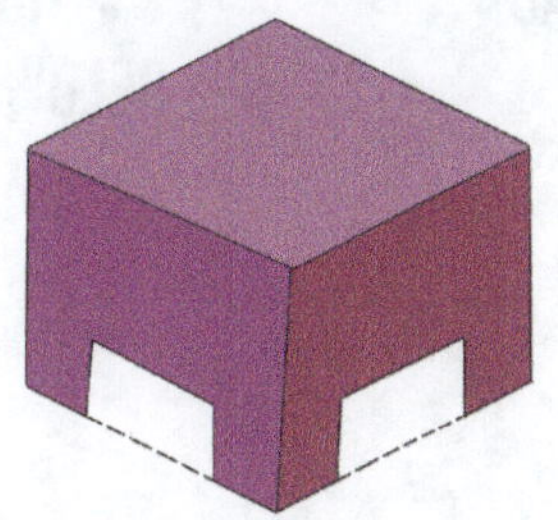 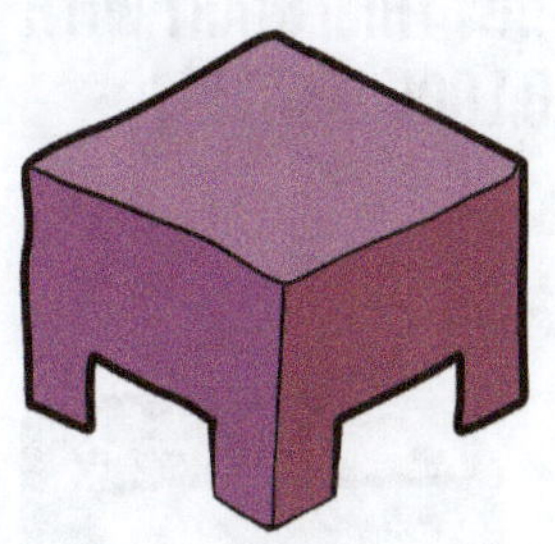

**2** NOW FOR THE LOWER PART, FOLLOW THE ILLUSTRATIONS BELOW. IT IS NOT THAT HARD.

 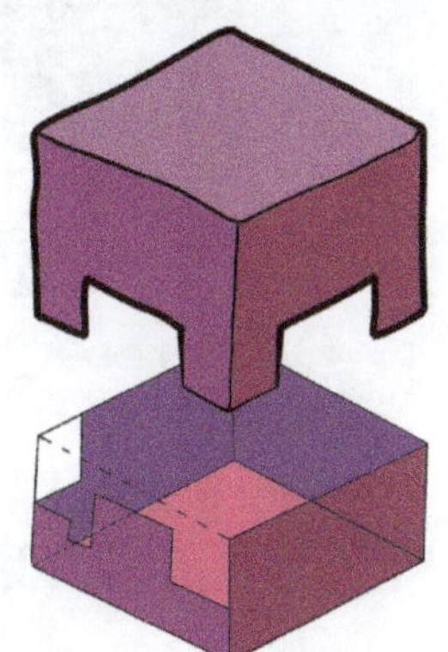 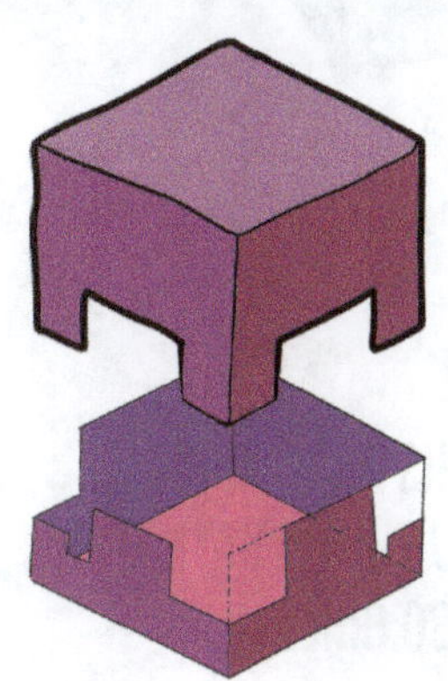 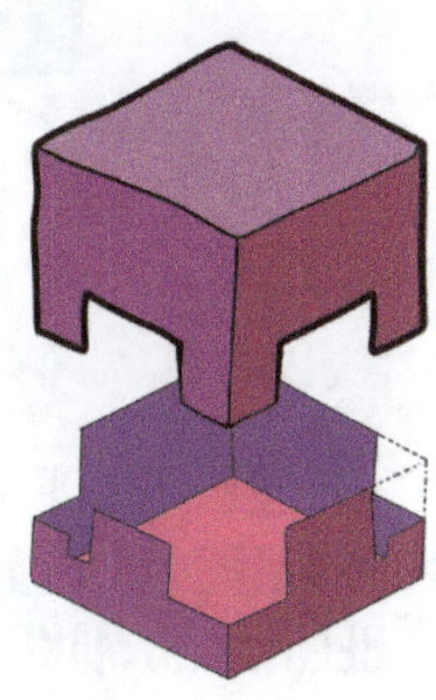

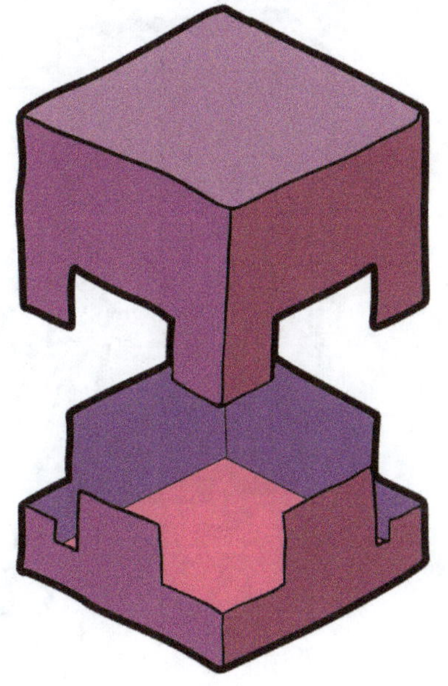

**3** USE THICKER LINES TO FORM THE FINAL SHAPE OF HIS SHELL. THIS IS HOW IT SHOULD LOOK LIKE.

# SKELETON

## 1

1. LET'S DRAW THIS! START WITH HIS HEAD AND IT SHOULD LOOK LIKE THIS:

## 2

NOW DRAW HIS TORSO, A SMALLER CUBE BELOW HIS HEAD.

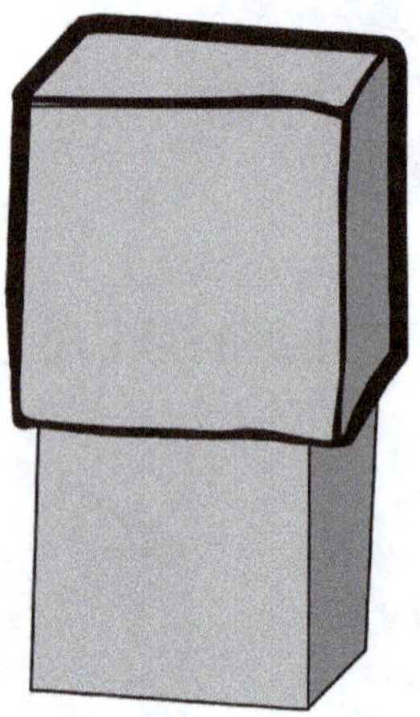

## 3

LET'S PROCEED WITH HIS ARM. AFTER DRAWING HIS ARM, FOLLOW THE ILLUSTRATION BELOW AND MAKE HIS TORSO BONY.

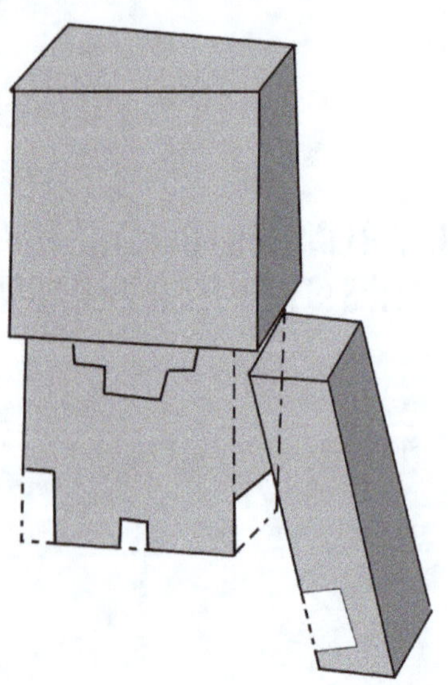

## 4

WHEN YOU ERASE ALL THE GUIDELINES, THIS IS HOW HIS TORSO SHOULD LOOK LIKE.

# SNOW GOLEM

**1** FOLLOW THESE EASY STEPS TO START SHAPING SNOW GOLEM'S HEAD AND UPPER BODY!

**2** NOW, DRAW HIS FULL BODY JUST LIKE THE DRAWING ON THE LEFT

**3** DRAW THIN LINES FOR HIS ARMS AND REMOVE LINE GUIDES.

**4** TO FINISH YOUR SNOW GOLEM, DRAW HIM A FACE AND SOME DETAILS ON HIS BODY. DOESN'T HE LOOK COOL?

# CREEPER



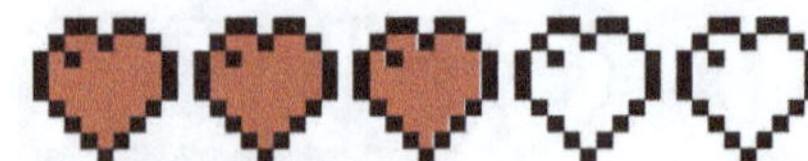

**1** 1. HEY, THIS ONE IS REALLY EASY TOO. THE CREEPER IS BASICALLY MADE FROM CUBES AND RECTANGULAR CUBOIDS. SO, LET'S START WITH DRAWING A CUBE FOR ITS HEAD AND A RECTANGULAR CUBOID FOR ITS BODY.

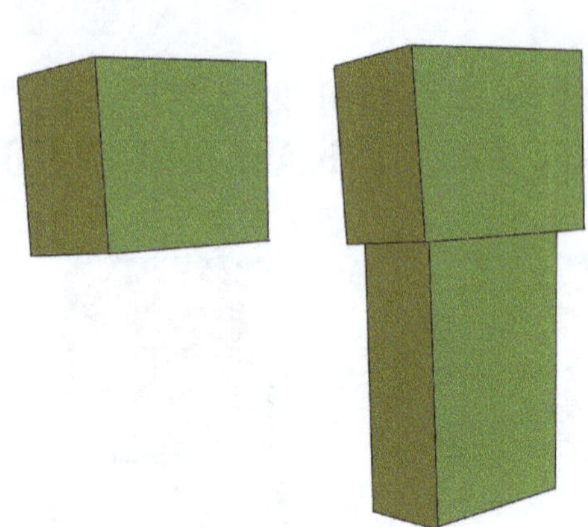

**2** 2. TO DRAW ITS LEGS, FOLLOW THESE STEPS: FIRST, DRAW A CUBE FOR ITS FIRST LEG. AFTER THAT DRAW TWO MORE CUBES. AT THIS POINT, YOU HAVE THE SHAPE OF ITS BODY.

**3** 3. ALMOST DONE! NOW YOU CAN FINISH YOUR DRAWING BY OUTLINING THE EDGES WITH THICKER LINES, ADDING ITS FACE, MOUTH AND SOME OTHER DETAILS WHICH WILL MAKE THE CREEPER LOOK SCARY.

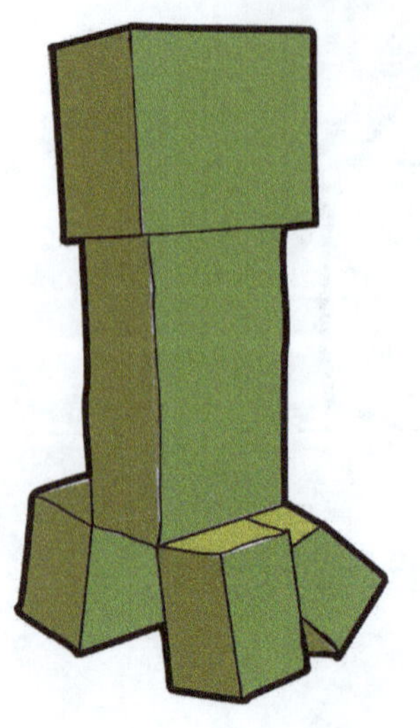

# STEVE

**1** START WITH THE SHAPE OF HIS HEAD.

**2** THEN DRAW HIS TORSO.

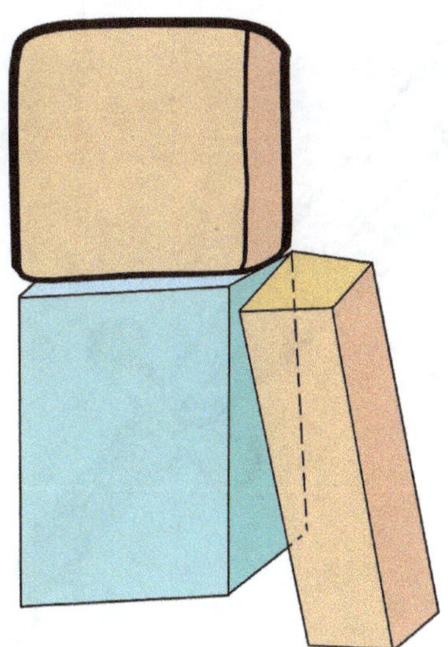

**3** NOW LET'S SHAPE HIS LEFT ARM.
FOLLOW THE DRAWING AND ERASE DOTTED LINES.

**4** LET'S DRAW HIS OTHER ARM. FIRST DRAW
AN ARM THEN SHAPE A PICKAXE.

# SWORD

**1** SHAPE A SWORD USING THESE THREE SHAPES.

**2** NOW, LET'S MAKE IT POINTY! FOLLOW THE DRAWING ABOVE AND FORM A SWORD.

**3** ADD LINES ON THE SWORD TO SEPARATE THE HANDLE FROM THE BLADE. ADD DETAILS ON ITS BLADE TO MAKE IT LOOK REALLY SHARP.

**4** ALMOST DONE! NOW YOU CAN FINISH YOUR DRAWING WITH SOME SMALL DETAILS ON THE HANDLE.

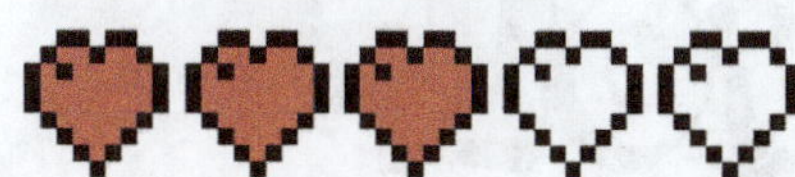

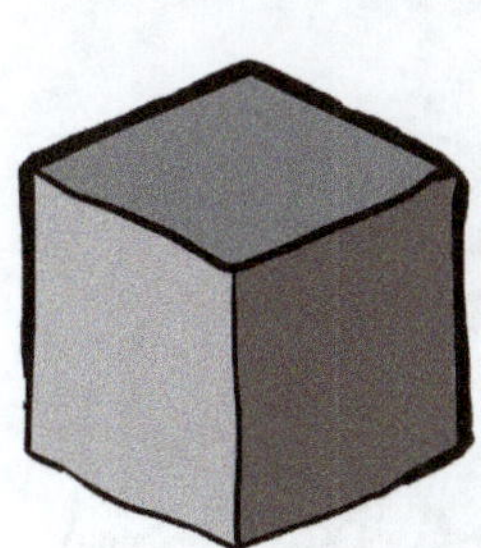

**1** OKAY, FIRST STEP IS EASY SO LET'S BEGIN! START WITH A CUBE FOR HIS HEAD.

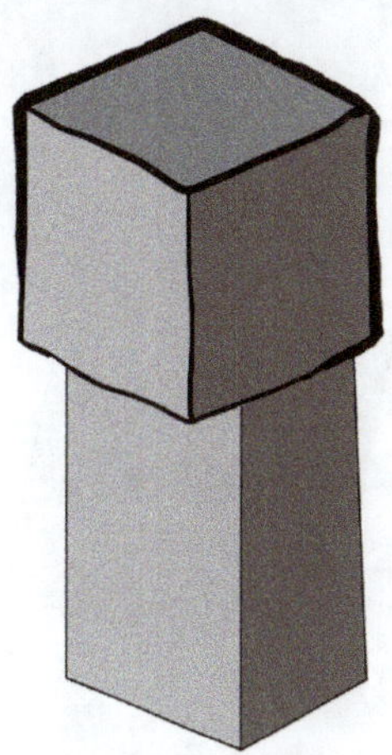

**2** NOW, DRAW HIM A TORSO.

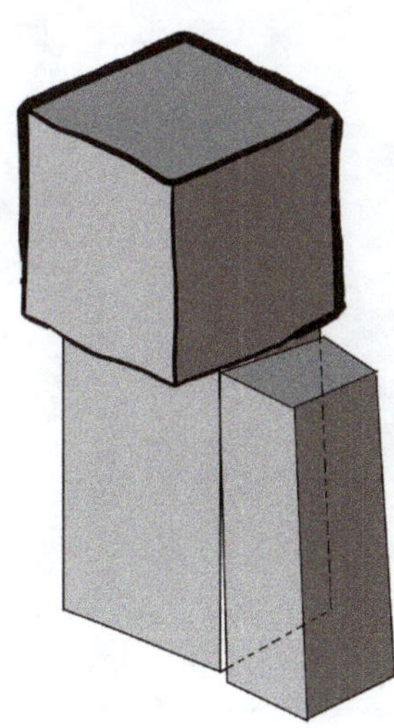

**3** NEXT STEP IS HIS LEFT ARM. DRAW SHAPE OF IT NEXT TO THE BODY.

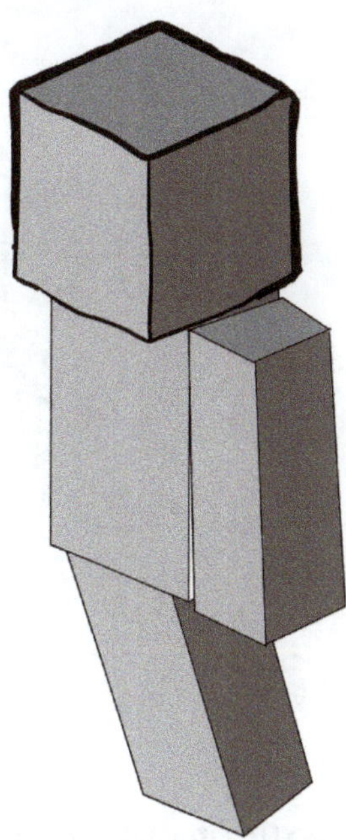

**4** WE CAN NOW DRAW HIM HIS LEGS FOLLOWING THE DRAWING ABOVE.

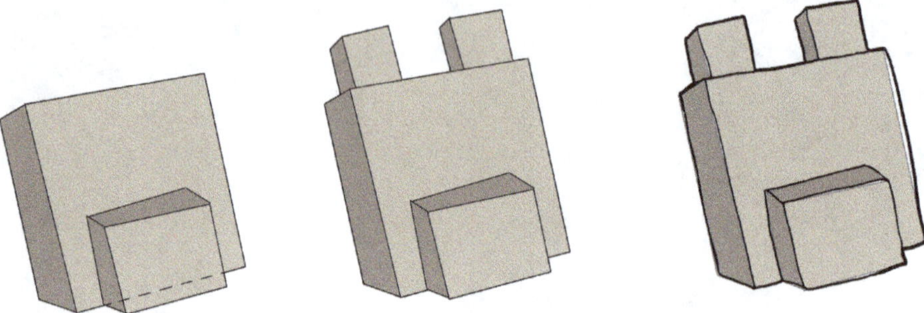

**1** FOLLOW THESE THREE EASY STEPS TO FORM THE WOLF'S HEAD. START WITH A BIG CUBE AND THEN DRAW SMALLER CUBES FOR HIS EARS AND MOUTH.

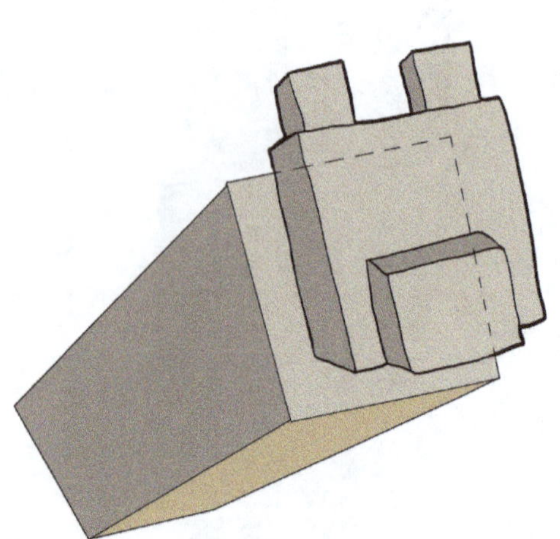

**2** FOLLOW THE DRAWING AND ADD HIM A TORSO.

**3** TO DRAW HIS FRONT LEGS, FOLLOW THE DRAWING ABOVE.

# ZOMBIE

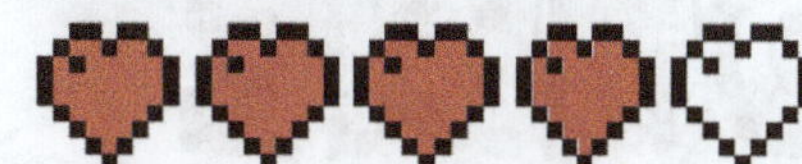

**1** TO START, DRAW A CUBE FOR HIS HEAD.

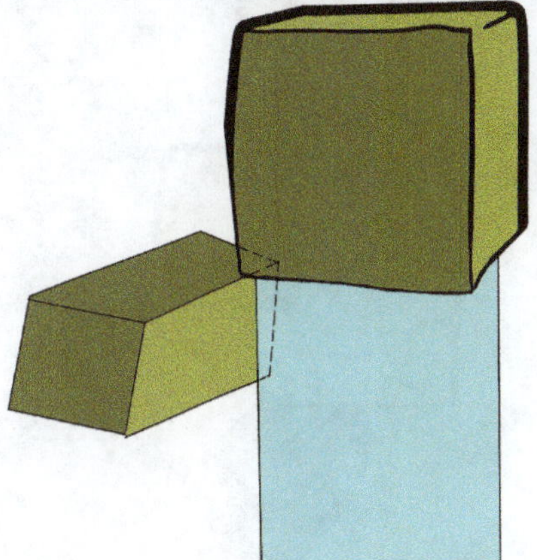

**2** DRAW A RECTANGLE FOR HIS TORSO AND SHAPE HIS RIGHT ARM.

**3** NOW, DRAW THE LEFT ARM AND THEN SHAPE HIS UPPER BODY WITH THICKER LINES.

# ZOMBIE

**4** DRAW ONE OF HIS LEGS.

**5** NOW YOU CAN SHAPE ANOTHER LEG FOLLOWING OUR DRAWING.

**6** NOW WHEN WE HAVE THE SHAPE OF HIS BODY, LET'S FINISH THE DRAWING.

**7** TO FINISH DRAWING THE ZOMBIE, MAKE HIS CLOTHES OLD AND DRAW HIS FACE WITH FEW SPOTS ON HIS HEAD.

# VINDICATOR



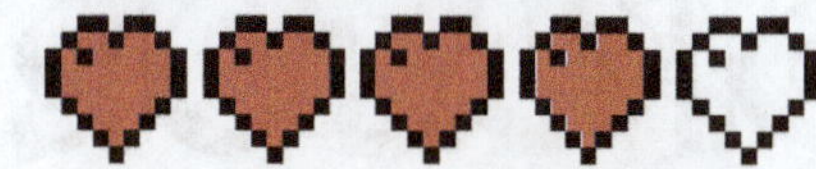

**1** START BY DRAWING A VERTICAL RECTANGULAR PRISM. SEPARATE HIS BODY AND HEAD BY ADDING A HORIZONTAL LINE ON THE UPPER PART OF THE PRISM. DRAW HIM HIS NOSE

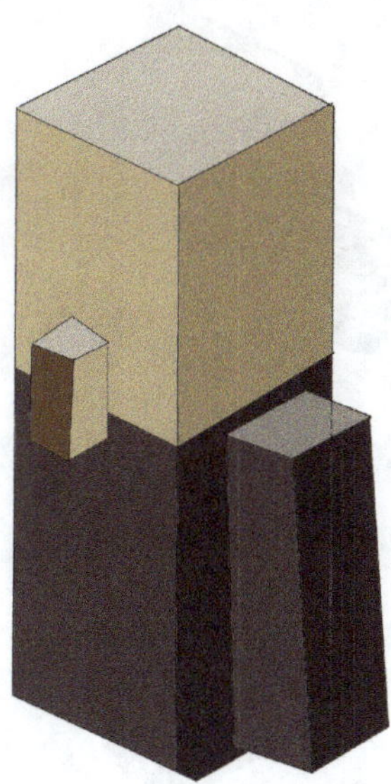

**2** DRAW THE SHAPE SHOWN ABOVE WHERE HIS ARM SHOULD BE.

**3** FOLLOW THE LINE GUIDES AND DRAW THE FINAL SHAPE OF HIS UPPER BODY IN A SUIT.

# VINDICATOR

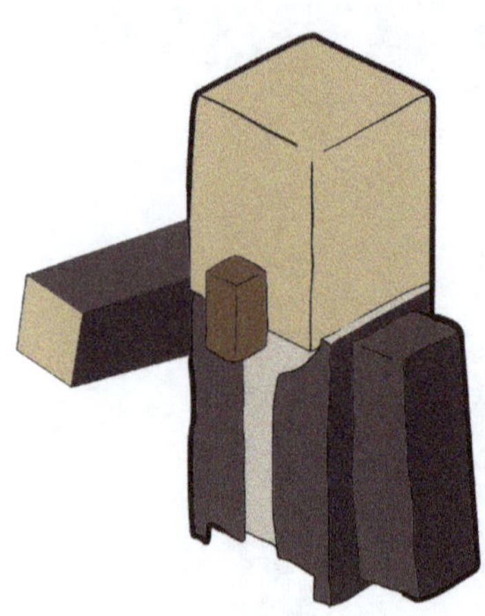

**4** NOW, DRAW THE SHAPE OF HIS OTHER ARM.

**5** NEXT STEP ARE LEGS AND A SHAPE OF AN AXE WHICH HE IS HOLDING.

**6** USE THICKER LINES TO DRAW THE FINAL SHAPE OF HIS LOWER BODY AND HIS AXE.

**7** TO FINISH THIS DRAWING, DRAW HIS FACE AND ADD DETAILS ON HIS CLOTHES.  USE SHADES AND THIN LINES TO MAKE HIM LOOK SCARY.

# WITCH

**1** LET'S START FROM THE TOP! TO DRAW WITCH HAT YOU SHOULD FOLLOW THESE STEPS:

  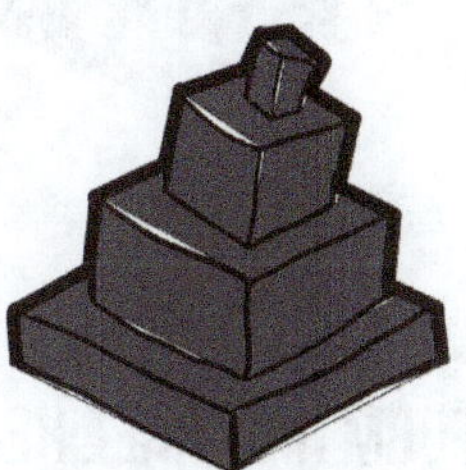

**2** NOW, DRAW A RECTANGULAR PRISM TO FORM HER BODY.

**3** SEPARATE HER BODY AND HEAD BY ADDING A HORIZONTAL LINE ON THE UPPER PART OF THE PRISM.

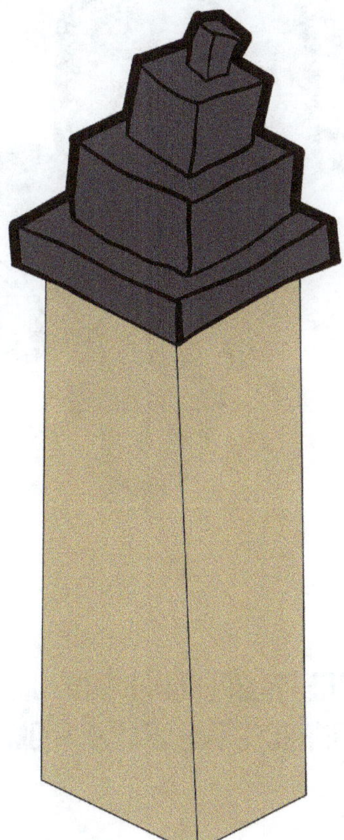

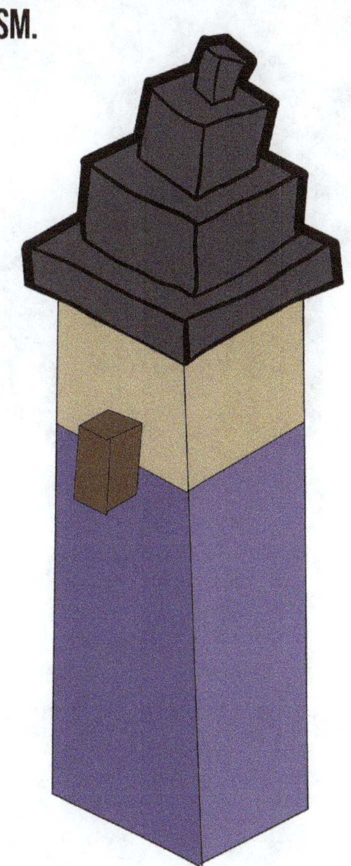

# WITHER

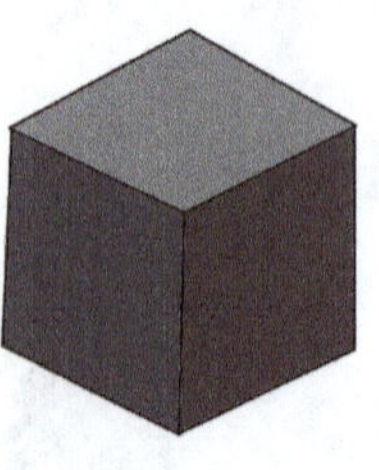
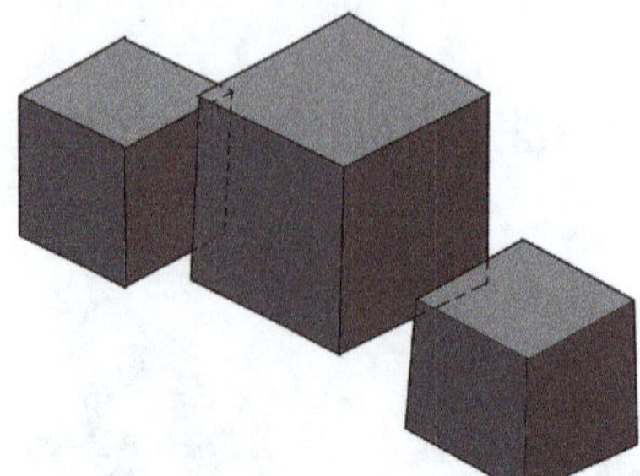

**1** FORM HIS THREE HEADS SIMPLY BY DRAWING THREE DIFFERENT CUBES STANDING IN LINE. USE OUR THIRD DRAWING TO CONNECT IT AND MAKE A FINAL FORM.

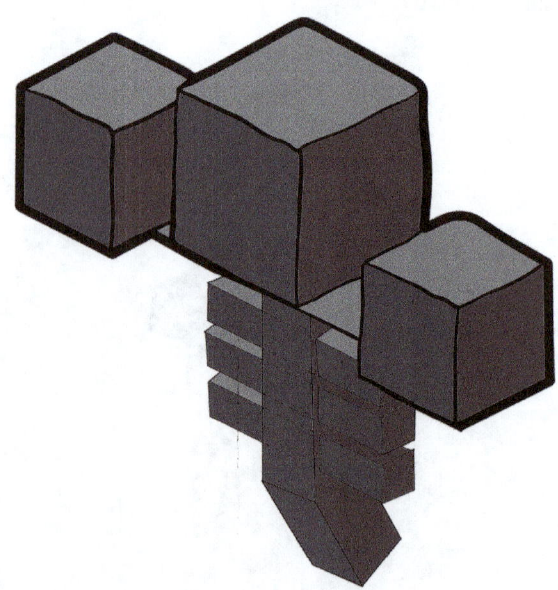

**2** FOLLOW THIS STEP AND START FORMING HIS TORSO.

**3** WE ARE PROGRESSING! NOW, DRAW A SHAPE WHICH CONNECTS THE SHAPES FROM STEP 2.

# WITHER

**5** ALMOST DONE! NOW WHEN YOU HAVE YOUR FINAL GUIDE, USE THICKER LINES TO DRAW HIM A FULL BODY.

**6** TO FINISH WITHER, DRAW HIM A FACE ON EACH HEAD. SHADING AND SOME DETAILS ON HIS BODY WILL MAKE HIM SUPER COOL!

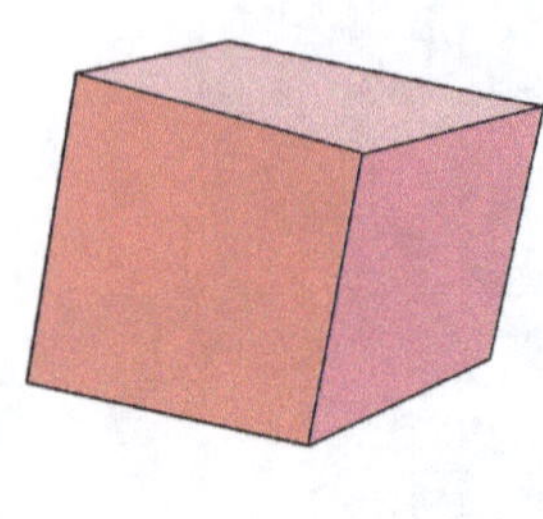
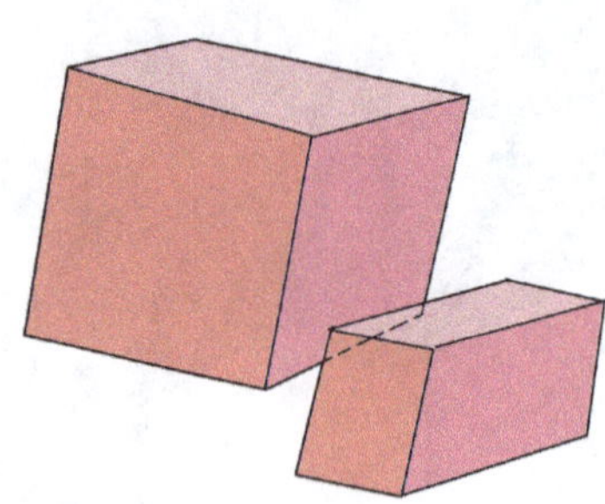
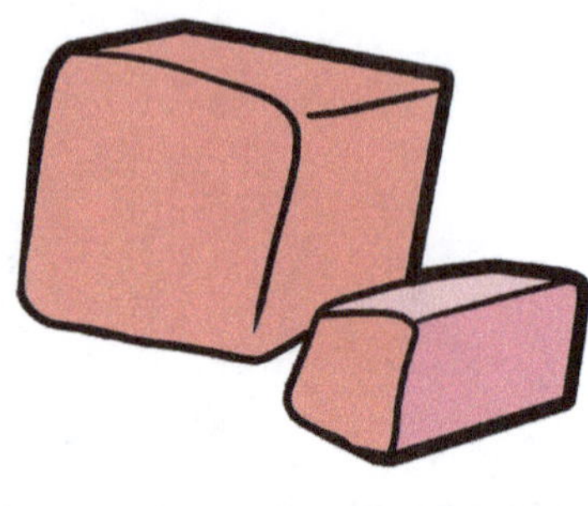

**1** FOLLOW THESE THREE SIMPLE STEPS TO FORM THE SHAPE OF HIS HEAD AND LEFT ARM.

**2** DRAW HIM A TORSO FOLLOWING THE IMAGE ABOVE.

**3** NOW DRAW HIS RIGHT ARM.

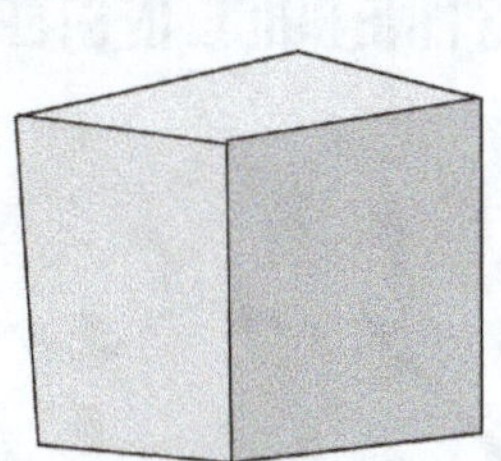

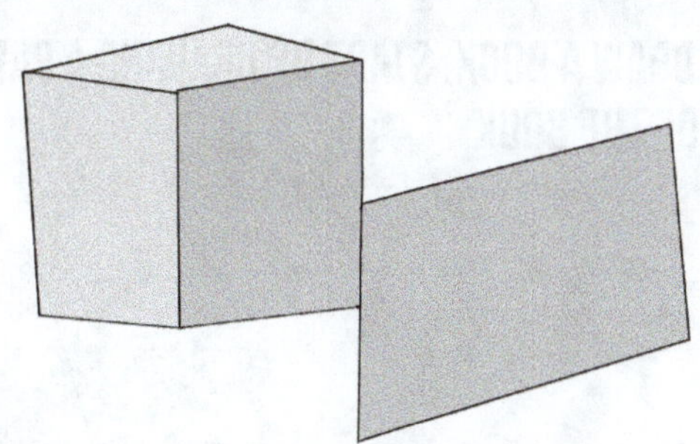

**1** DRAW A CUBE. THEN DRAW A RECTANGLE BESIDE THE CUBE AS SHOWN IN OUR GUIDE.

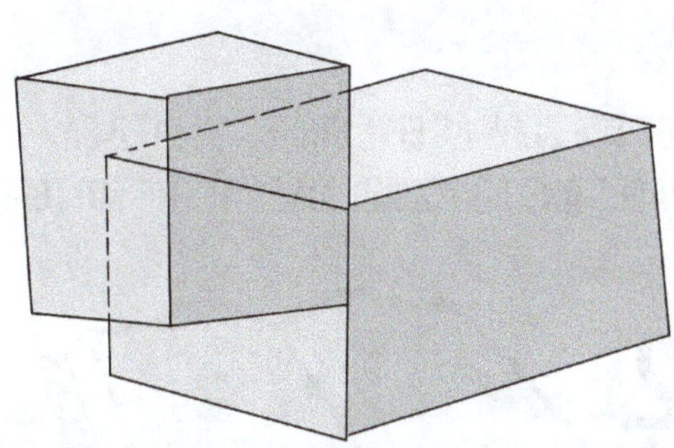

**2** NOW ADD DIMENSIONS TO THE RECTANGLE TO CREATE A CUBOID. ERASE DOTTED LINES.

**3** TO FORM SHEEP'S TORSO, FOLLOW THE GUIDE BELOW. DON'T WORRY, IT IS NOT THAT HARD. JUST RELAX AND FOLLOW THE DRAWING.

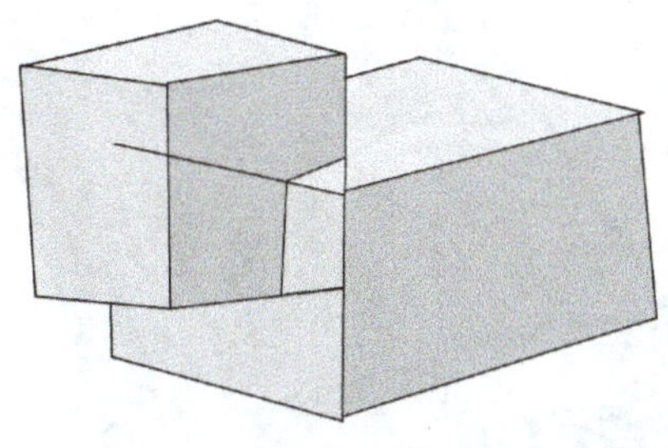

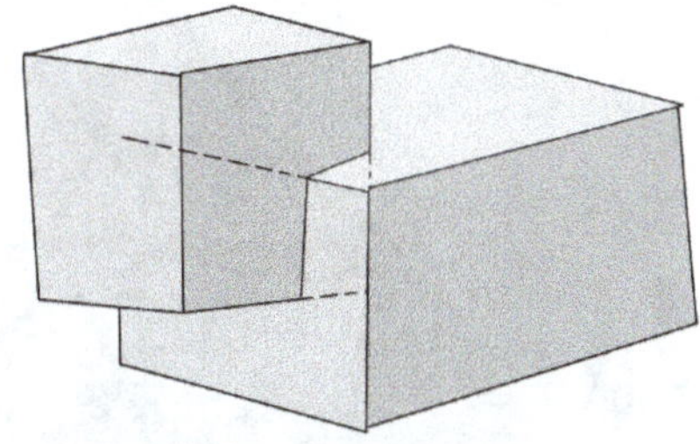

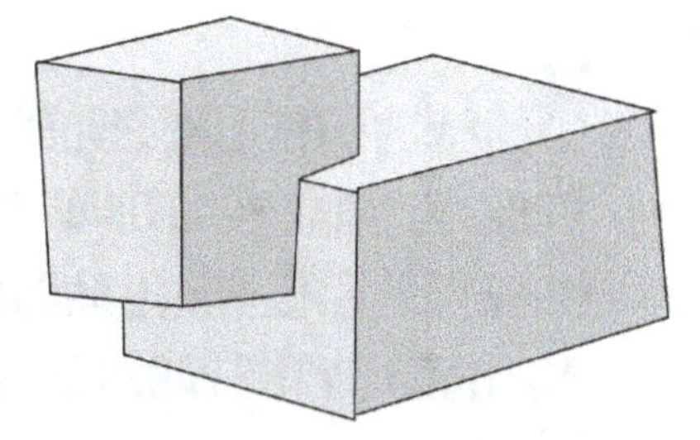

# BOOK

**1** LET'S DRAW A BOOK. START BY DRAWING A PARALLELOGRAM AS LINE GUIDE. IN STEP 1A, TRACE THE OUTLINE OF THE BOOK

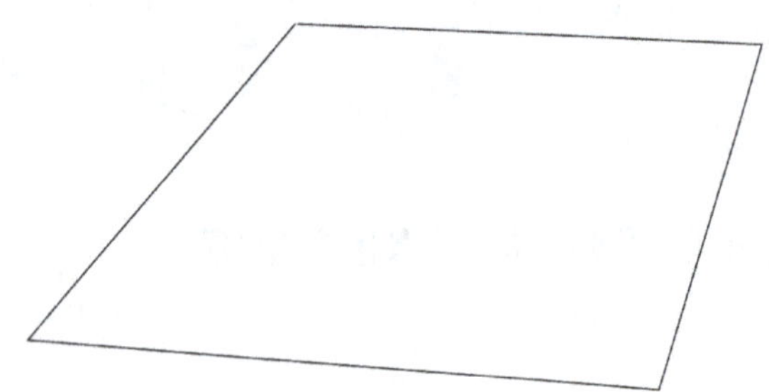

**2** DRAW A THIN CUBOID AT THE BOTTOM AND AT THE EDGE OF THE BOOK AS LINE GUIDES. IN STEP 2A, DRAW A MIDDLE VERTICAL LINE ON THE BOOK TO MAKE ITS PAGES AND ADD CURVE LINES AT THE BOTTOM.

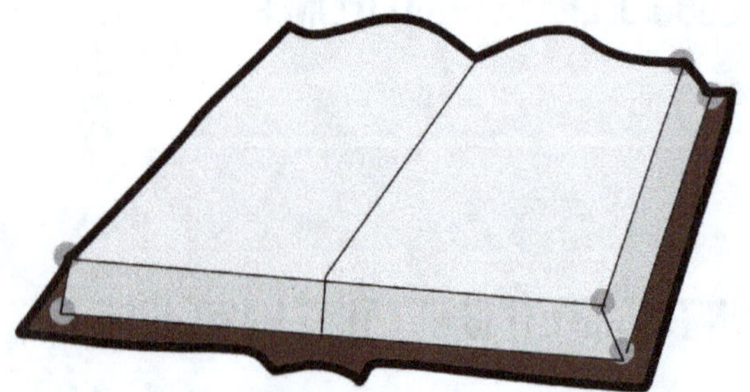

**3** REMOVE THE LINE GUIDES OF THE BOOK. TO MAKE YOUR DRAWING LOOK MORE REALISTIC, WRITE AND DRAW ANYTHING ON THE PAGES OF THE BOOK.

# POTION

**1** TO DRAW A POTION, START WITH A SHAPE OF A BOTTLE. TRY TO DRAW SOMETHING LIKE THIS:

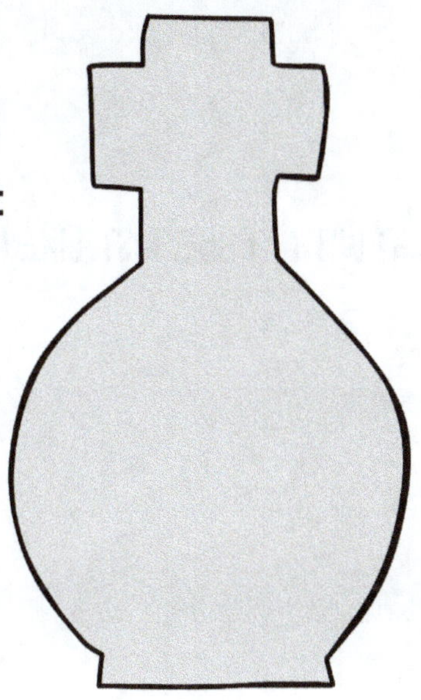

**2** SEPARATE THE BOTTLE FROM THE CORK. DRAW A SHADING OF A GLASS REFLECTION ON THE BOTTLE.

**3** YOU ARE ALMOST FINISHED! USE THINNER LINES TO DRAW SMALL DETAILS ON YOUR BOTTLE. COLOR IT AND THERE IT IS!

# JUKEBOX



**1** START WITH A CUBE, JUST  LIKE THIS ONE:

**2** DRAW THICKER LINES ON ITS EDGES AND HORIZONTAL LINES ON TOP OF THE CUBE.

**3** ALMOST DONE! FINISH OFF THIS DRAWING BY ADDING DETAILS ON THE BODY OF THE JUKEBOX

# ANVIL

**1** OKAY, THESE STEPS ARE EASY SO LET'S BEGIN. FIRST, DRAW A THIN RECTANGLE. DRAW ANOTHER RECTANGLE BELOW THE FIRST ONE BUT THIS RECTANGLE IS THICKER AS SHOWN IN IMAGE 1A. FEEL FREE TO REMOVE THE DOTTED LINES.

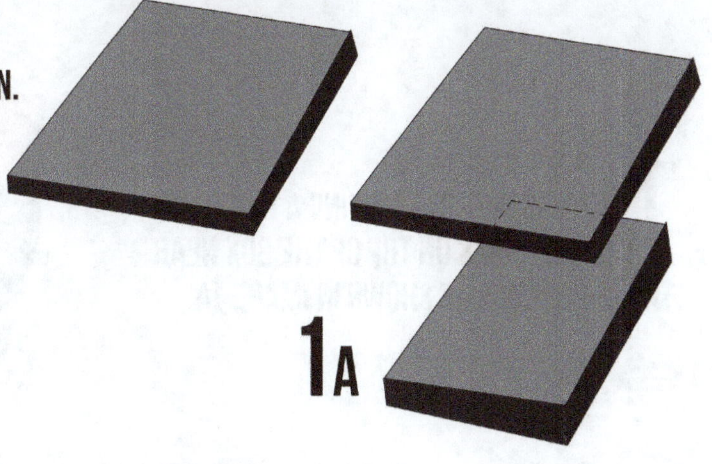



**2** DRAW TWO LINES CONNECTING YOUR TWO RECTANGLES TO FORM THE FINAL SHAPE OF YOUR ANVIL. ADD THE HORN OF THE ANVIL AS SHOWN IN 2A.

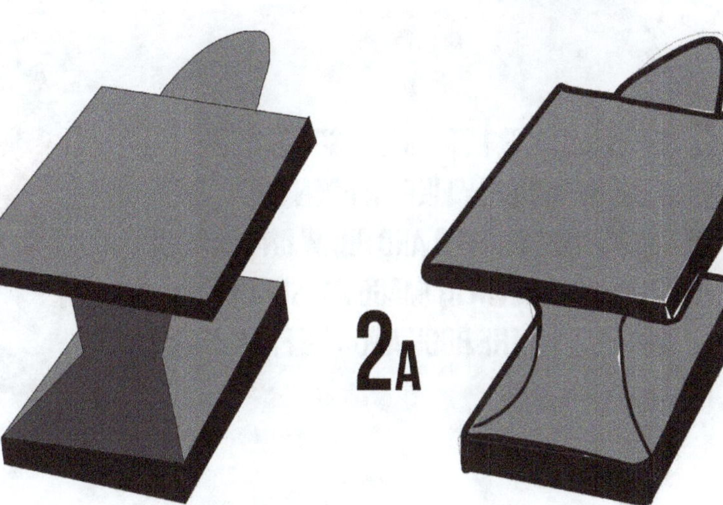

**3** ALMOST DONE! ADD SOME DETAILS ON YOUR ANVIL TO MAKE IT LOOK REALISTIC.

# ENCHANTMENT TABLE

**1** LET US START BY DRAWING A BOX. THEN ADD TWO CUBOIDS ON TOP OF THE BOX NEAR THE UPPER EDGE AS SHOWN IN IMAGE 1A.

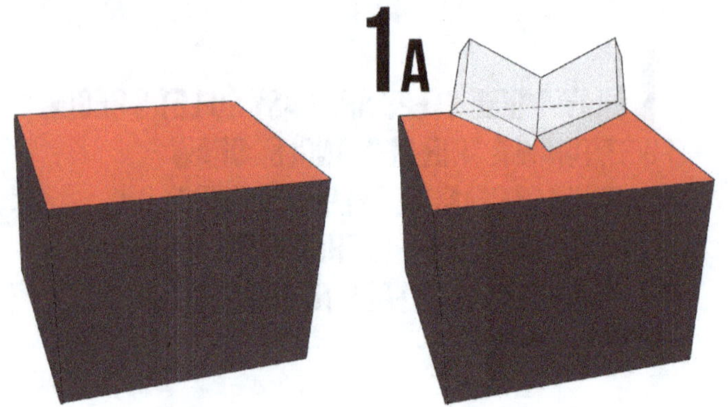

**2** AT THIS STAGE, LET'S DRAW SOMETHING THAT LOOKS ROUGHLY LIKE AN OPEN BOOK. THEN DRAW THE BOOK COVER AND DRAW ONE PAGE OF THE BOOK AS SHOWN IN IMAGE 2A. SHADE THE OUTER LINES OF THE BOOK AND THE ENCHANTMENT TABLE.

**3** ADD DETAILS ON YOUR ENCHANTMENT TABLE AND PUT WRITINGS OR DRAWINGS ON YOUR BOOK TO FINISH OFF THE IMAGE.

# CAKE

**1** OK, THIS IS EASY, SO LETS BEGIN!  DRAW THIS SHAPE:

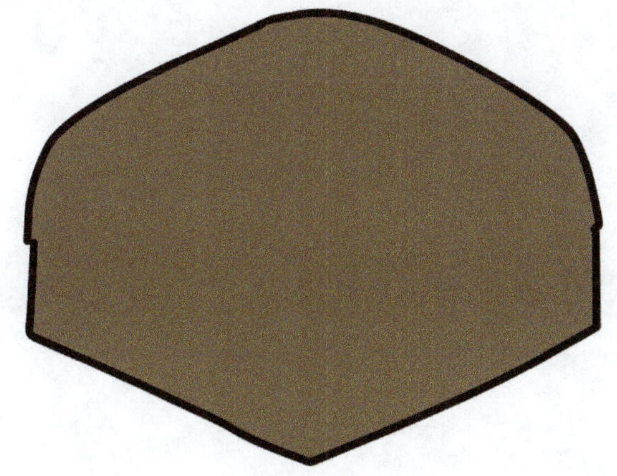

**2** NOW TO MAKE IT LOOK LIKE A CAKE, DRAW ITS SIDES AND ADD CREAM ON TOP.

**3** ALMOST DONE! ALL YOU HAVE TO DO IS DRAW A CANDLE AND ADD DETAILS AND SHADINGS ON YOUR CAKE.